teach®
yourself

instant portuguese
elisabeth smith

For over 60 years, more than
50 million people have learnt over
750 subjects the **teach yourself**
way, with impressive results.

be where you want to be
with **teach yourself**

For UK order enquiries: please contact Bookpoint Ltd, 130 Milton Park, Abingdon, Oxon OX14 4SB. Telephone: +44 (0) 1235 827720. Fax: +44 (0) 1235 400454. Lines are open 09.00–17.00, Monday to Saturday, with a 24-hour message answering service. Details about our titles and how to order are available at www.teachyourself.co.uk

For USA order enquiries: please contact McGraw-Hill Customer Services, PO Box 545, Blacklick, OH 43004-0545, USA. Telephone: 1-800-722-4726. Fax: 1-614-755-5645.

For Canada order enquiries: please contact McGraw-Hill Ryerson Ltd, 300 Water St, Whitby, Ontario L1N 9B6, Canada. Telephone: 905 430 5000. Fax: 905 430 5020.

Long renowned as the authoritative source for self-guided learning – with more than 50 million copies sold worldwide – the **teach yourself** series includes over 500 titles in the fields of languages, crafts, hobbies, business, computing and education.

British Library Cataloguing in Publication Data: a catalogue record for this title is available from the British Library.

Library of Congress Catalog Card Number: on file.

First published in UK 2000 by Hodder Education, 338 Euston Road, London, NW1 3BH.

First published in US 2000 by The McGraw-Hill Companies, Inc.

2nd edition published 2003. 3rd edition published 2006.

The **teach yourself** name is a registered trade mark of Hodder Headline.

Typeset by Transet Limited, Coventry, England.
Printed in Great Britain for Hodder Education, a division of Hodder Headline, 338 Euston Road, London, NW1 3BH, by Cox & Wyman Ltd, Reading, Berkshire.

Hodder Headline's policy is to use papers that are natural, renewable and recyclable products and made from wood grown in sustainable forests. The logging and manufacturing processes are expected to conform to the environmental regulations of the country of origin.

Impression number   10 9 8 7 6 5 4 3 2 1
Year   2010 2009 2008 2007 2006

contents

If, like me, you usually skip introductions, don't! Read on! You need to know how **Instant Portuguese** works and why.

When I decided to write the **Instant** series I first called it *Barebones*, because that's what you want: *no frills, no fuss, just the bare bones and go!* So in **Instant Portuguese** you'll find:

- 396 words to say everything, well... nearly everything.

- No ghastly grammar – just a few useful tips.

- No time wasters such as 'the pen of my aunt...'

- No phrase for when you lose a crown from your front tooth while doing the city tour of Lisbon.

- No need to be perfect. Mistakes won't spoil your success.

I've put some 30 years of teaching experience into this course. I know how people learn. I also know how long they are motivated by a new project (a few weeks) and how little time they can spare to study each day (½ hour). That's why you'll complete **Instant Portuguese** in six weeks and get away with 35 minutes a day.

Of course there is some learning to do, but I have tried to make it as much fun as possible, even when it is boring. You'll meet Tom and Kate Walker on holiday in Portugal. They do the kind of things you need to know about: shopping, eating out and getting about. As you will note Tom and Kate speak **Instant Portuguese** all the time, even to each other. What paragons of virtue!

To get the most out of this course, there are only two things you really should do:

- Follow the **Day-by-day guide** as suggested. Please don't skip bits and short-change your success. Everything is there for a reason.
- If you are a complete beginner, buy the recording that accompanies this book. It will help you to speak faster and with confidence.

When you have filled in your **Certificate** at the end of the book and can speak **Instant Portuguese**, I would like to hear from you. Why not visit my website www.elisabeth-smith.co.uk, e-mail me at elisabeth.smith@hodder.co.uk, or write to me care of Hodder Education, 338 Euston Road, London, NW1 3BH?

Elisabeth Smith

how this book works

Instant Portuguese has been structured for your rapid success. This is how it works:

Day-by-day guide Stick to it. If you miss a day, add one.

Dialogues Follow Tom and Kate through Portugal. The English of Weeks 1–3 is in 'Portuguese-speak' to get you tuned in.

New words Don't fight them, don't skip them – learn them! The flash cards will help you.

Good news grammar After you read it you can forget half and still succeed! That's why it's good news.

Flash words and flash sentences Read about these building blocks in the flash card section on page 92. Then use them!

Learn by heart Obligatory! Memorizing puts you on the fast track to speaking in full sentences.

Let's speak Portuguese *You* will be doing the talking – in Portuguese. Best with the recording.

Spot the keys Listen to rapid Portuguese and make sense of it.

Say it simply Learn how to use plain, **Instant Portuguese** to say what you want to say. Don't be shy!

Test your progress Mark your own test and be amazed by the result.

Answers This is where you'll find the answers to the exercises.

▶ This icon asks you to switch on the recording.

Pronunciation If you don't know it and don't have the recording go straight to page 15. You need to know about pronunciation before you can start Week 1.

Progress chart Enter your score each week and monitor your progress. Are you going for *very good* or *outstanding*?

Certificate It's on the last page. In six weeks it will have your name on it!

At the end of each week record your test score on the Progress chart below.

At the end of the course throw out your worst result – anybody can have a bad week – and add up your *five* best weekly scores. Divide the total by five to get your average score and overall course result.

Write your result – *outstanding, excellent, very good* or *good* – on your **Certificate** at the end of the book. If you scored more than 80% enlarge it and frame it!

Progress chart

90–100%							outstanding
80–89%							excellent
70–79%							very good
60–69%							good
Weeks	1	2	3	4	5	6	

Total of five best weeks =

divided by five =

Your final result _____ %

01

week one

Day zero

- Open the book and read **Read this first.**
- Now read **How this book works.**

Day one

- Read **In the aeroplane.**
- Listen to/Read **No avião.**
- Listen to/Read the **New words,** then learn some of them.

Day two

- Repeat **No avião** and the **New words.**
- Listen to/Read **Pronunciation.**
- Learn more **New words.**

Day three

- Learn all the **New words** until you know them well.
- Cut out the 22 **Flash words** and use them to help you.
- Read and learn the **Good news grammar.**

Day four

- Cut out and learn the **Flash sentences.**
- Listen to/Read **Learn by heart.**

Day five

- Listen to/Read **Let's speak Portuguese.**
- Revise! Tomorrow you'll be testing your progress.

Day six

- Listen to/Read **Let's speak more Portuguese** (optional).
- Listen to/Read **Let's speak Portuguese – fast and fluently** (optional).
- Translate **Test your progress.**

Day seven is your day off!

day-by-day guide

In the aeroplane

Tom and Kate Walker are on their way to Portugal. They are boarding flight TAP 701 to Faro via Lisbon and squeeze past Paulo Boa-morte. (*The English of Weeks 1–3 is in 'Portuguese-speak' to get you tuned in.*)

Tom	Excuse me, we have (the) seats 9a and 9b.
Paulo	Oh yes, a moment please.
Tom	Hello. I am Tom Walker and this is my wife, Kate.
Paulo	Good day. My name is Boa-morte.
Tom	Luís Boa-morte, the footballer?
Paulo	No, unfortunately not! I am called Paulo Boa-morte.
Tom	We are going to Faro. And you, (Sir)?
Paulo	Well, I am going to Lisbon, but I am from (the) Porto.
Tom	From (the) Porto? Well, I was in (the) Porto in May. It is very lovely. I was there for my work.
Paulo	What is it that you do?
Tom	I work in computing. I work for (the) Unilever.
Paulo	And you? What is it that you do?
Kate	I worked in a travel agency. I now work for (the) Rover. It is better.
Paulo	Are you from London?
Kate	No, we are from Manchester. We were three years in London and a year in New York. Now we work in Birmingham.
Paulo	I worked for (the) Shell. Now I am at the Bank of Portugal.
Tom	How is the work at the bank? Good?
Paulo	The job is boring, but the money is good. I have a house big, a Mercedes and four children. My wife is American. She has parents in Los Angeles and a girl-friend in Florida and is always on the telephone. It costs a lot of money!
Kate	Now we are on holiday. You, (Sir) too?
Paulo	Unfortunately not. We have holidays in September. We are going to Madeira – but without the children. We have there a house without telephone, and we go there without mobile!

▶ No avião

Tom and Kate Walker are on their way to Portugal. They are boarding flight TAP 701 to Faro via Lisbon and squeeze past Paulo Boa-morte.

Tom   Desculpe, temos os lugares nove a e nove b.

Paulo Ah sim, um momento se faz favor.

Tom   Olá. Sou Tom Walker e esta é a minha esposa, Kate.

Paulo Bom dia. O meu nome é Boa-morte.

Tom   Luís Boa-morte, o futebolista?

Paulo Não, infelizmente não! Chamo-me Paulo Boa-morte.

Tom   Nós vamos para Faro, e o senhor?

Paulo Pois, eu vou para Lisboa, mas sou do Porto.

Tom   Do Porto? Pois estive no Porto em Maio. É muito bonito. Estive lá em trabalho.

Paulo O que é que faz?

Tom   Trabalho em informática. Trabalho para a Unilever.

Paulo E a senhora, o que é que faz?

Kate   Trabalhava numa agência de viagens. Agora trabalho para a Rover. É melhor.

Paulo São de Londres?

Kate   Não, somos de Manchester. Estivemos três anos em Londres e um ano em Nova Iorque. Agora trabalhamos em Birmingham.

Paulo Eu trabalhei para a Shell. Agora estou no Banco de Portugal.

Tom   Como é o trabalho no banco? Bom?

Paulo O trabalho é chato, mas o dinheiro é bom. Tenho uma casa grande, um Mercedes e quatro filhos. A minha esposa é americana. Tem os pais em Los Ângeles, e uma amiga na Florida e está sempre ao telefone. Custa muito dinheiro!

Kate   Agora estamos de férias. O senhor também?

Paulo Infelizmente não. Temos férias em Setembro. Vamos para a Madeira, mas sem os filhos. Temos lá uma casa sem telefone, e vamos para lá sem telemóvel!

▶ New words

em; no, na *in, on/in, on the*
o avião *the aeroplane*
desculpe *excuse me*
temos *we have*
os lugares *the seats*
a, b say *'uh', 'bay'*
e *and*
sim *yes*
um momento *a moment*
se faz favor *please (if you please)*
olá *hello*
sou *I am*
este/esta/isto *this* (by itself)
é *is*
a minha esposa *my wife*
bom dia *good day, good morning*
o meu nome é... *my name is...*
não *no, not*
infelizmente *unfortunately*
chamo-me *I am called*
nós *we*
vamos *we go/are going, let's go!*
para *to, for*
o/a/os/as *the*
o senhor/a senhora *you* (sing. male/female) also *Sir, Mr, the gentleman/Madam, Mrs, the lady*
pois... *well...*
eu *I*
vou *I go/am going*
mas *but*
de; do, da *from, of; from the, of the*
estive *I was/have been*
Maio *May*
é *he/she/it is, you* (sing.) *are*
muito *very, much, a lot*
bonito/a *pretty, lovely*
lá *there*
em trabalho *on business, for my company*
o trabalho *the work*
o que *what, that*
o que é que faz? *what do you do?*
trabalho *I work*
a informática *the computing*
(o computador) *(the computer)*
(trabalhei), trabalhava *(I (have) worked), I was working*
numa *in a*
a agência de viagens *the travel agency*
agora *now*
melhor *better*
são *you* (pl.)/*they are*
somos *we are*
estivemos *we were*
três *three*
o ano, os anos *the year, the years*
um/uma *a, one*
trabalhamos *we work*
estou *I am*
o Banco de Portugal *the Bank of Portugal*
como *how*
bom/boa *good*
chato/a *boring*
o dinheiro *the money*
tenho *I have*
uma casa *a house*
grande *big*
quatro *four*
os filhos *the children*
americano/a *American*
tem *he/she/it has, you* (sing.) *have*
os pais *the parents*
uma amiga *a (female) friend*
está *is*
sempre *always*

ao telefone	*on the telephone*	**Setembro**	*September*
custa	*it costs*	**sem**	*without*
estamos	*we are*	**o telefone, telefonar**	*the*
de férias	*on holiday(s)*		*telephone, to telephone*
também	*also, too*	**o telemóvel**	*the mobile phone*

> **TOTAL NEW WORDS: 80**
> **...only 316 words to go!**

Some easy extras

Os meses (the months of the year)

Janeiro, Fevereiro, Março, Abril, Maio, Junho, Julho, Agosto, Setembro, Outubro, Novembro, Dezembro

Números (numbers)

zero,	um/uma,	dois/duas,	três,	quatro,	cinco,	seis,	sete,	oito,	nove,	dez
0	1	2	3	4	5	6	7	8	9	10

More greetings

boa tarde *good afternoon*, **boa noite** *good evening/night*, **até logo** *bye, until later*, **adeus** *goodbye* (for longer absence).

▶ Pronunciation

If Portuguese pronunciation is new to you, please buy the recording. But if you are good at languages, or would like a refresher, here are the basic rules:

First the vowels

The word in brackets gives you an example of the sound. Say the sound OUT LOUD and then the Portuguese examples OUT LOUD.

a	(*star, asleep*)	v*a*mos, p*a*ra, m*a*s, c*a*sa
e	(*best*)	*é*, tr*ê*s, t*e*mos, s*e*mpre
i	(*field*)	est*i*ve, d*i*a, bon*i*to
o	(*not, moon*)	s*o*mos, c*o*mo
u	(*June*)	desc*u*lpe, l*u*gares, n*u*ma

Nasal vowels

When you see a little squiggle on top of a vowel, it changes the 'clean' vowel into a nasal one – as if you added 'ng' after it and had a cold at the same time. Now hold your nose and say: **não** ('naong').

An -m at the end also changes a 'clean' vowel into a nasal: **sim** ('sing'), **bom** ('bong'), **um** ('oong').

Doubles

When you see two or more vowels together you pronounce them all, as described above. So **euro** is pronounced 'eh-oo-roo'.

Consonants

These are the same as in English, except for the following:

c (cidade)	before *e* or *i* – like the English *s* in *seat*
ç (conheço)	When you spot a little hook under a **c** it also tells you to pronounce the **c** like the English *s* in *seat*.
ch (chato)	like the English *sh* in *shoot*
g (agência)	before *e* or *i* – a soft slurring sound like the *s* in *treasure*
h (hotel)	silent
j (Janeiro)	softly slurring like the *s* in *treasure*
lh (melhor)	like the *ll* in *million*
nh (tenho)	like the *ny* in *canyon*
qu (quilo)	before *e* or *i* – like the *k* in *kettle*
r (para)	give this a roll
rr (carro)	give this a vigorous roll: 'rrrr'
s (casa)	between vowels – like the English *z* in *zoo*
(férias)	before consonants and at ends of words – like the English *sh* in *shoot*
x (caixa)	sometimes like the English *sh* in *shoot*
(exemplo)	sometimes like the English *z* in *zoo*
(próximo)	sometimes like the English *s* in *seat*
z (fazer)	like the English *z*, except at ends of words
(faz)	when it is like the English *sh*. You'll pick it up as you go along.

Stress

Always stress the second syllable from the end: **mo-*men*-to, a-me-ri-*ca*-na**, unless the word ends in a consonant other than -am, -em or -s, when you should stress the last syllable instead: **Por-tu-*gal*.**

When there's an accent, stress that part: **in-for-*má*-ti-ca, a-*gên*-cia**.

Congratulations on working through the basic rules of Portuguese pronunciation!

If you'd like to hear the real thing and lots more, do treat yourself to the recording.

▶ Good news grammar

Remember, I promised? No ghastly grammar! Every week I just explain a few things, especially the differences between English and Portuguese. This will help you to speak Portuguese **Instantly!**

1 Names of things – nouns

There are two kinds of nouns in Portuguese – masculine and feminine. This means that there are two ways of saying *the* or *a* when you talk about things.

You use **o** and **um** for masculine nouns and **a** and **uma** for feminine nouns.

o dinheiro *the money*	*um* banco *a bank*
a casa *the house*	*uma* ami*ga a (female) friend*

Often the ending of the noun tells you if it is masculine or feminine.

For example, if the ending is -o, like in **banco**, it is usually masculine, but if it is -a, like in **casa**, it is normally feminine. The adjective which describes the noun frequently 'rhymes along' with the same ending: **um ano chato, uma casa bonita**.

Unfortunately, many other nouns and adjectives have endings which don't give you a clue as to whether they're masculine or feminine, like **telefone** or **grande** or **bom**. But don't worry – you'll pick these up as you go along.

When you talk about more than one thing, **o** becomes **os**, **a** becomes **as**, and the noun usually just gets an -s at the end: **os filhos** – *the children*, **as senhoras** – *the ladies*. But words ending in -m change the -m to -n before adding the -s: **bom – bons**. Easy enough!

Best of all: if you muddle things up and say *um* **casa** or *a* **dinheiro** nobody will throw a fit – everyone will understand you perfectly!

2 Doing things – verbs

First the bad news: verb drill – just like school! Unfortunately, there is just no 'quick fix' to memorize verb endings.

Have a look at the two 'gift boxes' on the next page and the list of six different persons doing something. As you can see in English there is only one small change to the verb *work*: he, she, or it *works*. But in Portuguese there are four different verb endings – depending on who is doing something.

Now for the good news. Once you know the endings of **trabalhar** (a 'regular' verb, a member of the Good Verbs Team) you can use the same endings with all other regular -**ar** verbs. And even **ter** (not a team member) has a similar sort of pattern. So it's not that bad. Say the verbs out loud, say them with your eyes closed, then say them backwards. Ten minutes for each box will do it.

trabalhar *(to) work*	
(eu) trabalh**o**	*I work*
(o senhor/a senhora)	
trabalh**a**	*you* (sing.) *work*
(ele/ela) trabalh**a**	*he, she, it works*
(nós) trabalh**amos**	*we work*
(os/as senhores/as)	
trabalh**am**	*you* (pl.) *work*
(eles, elas) trabalh**am**	*they work*

ter *(to) have*	
(eu) tenho	*I have*
(o senhor/a senhora)	
tem	*you* (sing.) *have*
(ele/ela) tem	*he, she, it has*
(nós) temos	*we have*
(os/as senhores/as)	
têm	*you* (pl.) *have*
(eles, elas) têm	*they have*

'I' and 'we': **eu** and **nós** – When the Portuguese say '*I am doing something*' or '*We are doing something*' they usually drop the **eu** and **nós**. So *I work* is **trabalho** and *we have* is **temos**, unless you want to stress that it is 'I' or 'we' who are doing something.

'You': **o senhor/a senhora** – There are several ways to say 'you' in Portuguese. **O senhor/a senhora** and **os senhores/as senhoras** is the polite and formal way used when addressing one or several other adults, especially strangers. Sounds grand, doesn't it? When you start making friends you can address them as **você** or **vocês** – as opposed to **o senhor/a senhora** – and use their first names. **Você** and **vocês** use the same verb endings as **o senhor/a senhora** and **os senhores/as senhoras**:

Luís, você trabalha para a Unilever?

Another way of saying *you* is **tu**, plural **vós**. This uses lots more complicated grammar, and you don't need it for **Instant Portuguese**!

▶ Let's speak Portuguese

I'll give you ten English sentences and you say them in Portuguese. Always speak OUT LOUD. After each one, check the answer at the bottom of the page and tick each sentence that you get right. If you have the recording, listen to check your answers to **Let's speak Portuguese**.

1 Good day. My name is Walker.
2 Are you from London?
3 Yes, I am from London.
4 We are going to Porto. Good-bye.
5 I work with Paulo in Estoril.
6 Do you have a Mercedes?
7 No, unfortunately not.
8 We have a house in Lagos.
9 How is the work at Shell? Good?
10 Boring, but the pay is good.

Well, how many did you get right? If you are not happy, do them again.

Here are some questions in Portuguese and you are going to answer in Portuguese. Answer the first five with **Sim**, and talk about yourself. In questions 16–20 I am talking to you and your friend. Say **Sim** and 'we'.

11 É de Bristol?
12 Tem casa em Londres?
13 O Paulo é de Lisboa. E o senhor / a senhora?
14 Tem telefone?
15 Trabalha em informática?
16 Vamos para Lisboa. E os senhores / e as senhoras?
17 Trabalhamos em Los Ângeles. E os senhores / e as senhoras?
18 Temos amigos em Faro. E os senhores / e as senhoras?
19 Vamos para Portimão. E os senhores / e as senhoras?
20 Temos um trabalho chato. E os senhores / e as senhoras?

Well, what was your score? If it was 20/20, give yourself a triple star!

Answers

1 Bom dia. O meu nome é Walker.
2 É de Londres?
3 Sim, sou de Londres.
4 Vamos para o Porto. Adeus.
5 Trabalho com o Paulo no Estoril.
6 Tem um Mercedes?
7 Não, infelizmente não.
8 Temos uma casa em Lagos.
9 Como é o trabalho na Shell, bom?
10 Chato, mas o dinheiro é bom.
11 Sim, sou de Bristol.
12 Sim, tenho casa em Londres.
13 Sim, sou de Lisboa.
14 Sim, tenho telefone.
15 Sim, trabalho em informática.
16 Sim, vamos para Lisboa.
17 Sim, trabalhamos em Los Ângeles.
18 Sim, temos amigos em Faro.
19 Sim, vamos para Portimão.
20 Sim, temos um trabalho chato.

▶ Let's speak more Portuguese

Here are some optional exercises. They may stretch the 35 minutes a day by 15 minutes. But the extra practice will be worth it.

And always remember: near enough is good enough!

In your own words

This exercise will teach you to express yourself freely. Use only the words you have learned so far.

Tell me in your own words that...

Example you are Peter Smith
Sou Peter Smith.

1 you are from Manchester
2 you have an American friend
3 you are a workaholic...
4 but you don't have a lot of cash
5 you have two children
6 the children are six and eight (have six and eight years)
7 unfortunately you work with a PC; it's boring
8 your wife works for a company in Bath
9 you own a property in Faro
10 you have holidays in April

Answers

1 Sou de Manchester.
2 Tenho um amigo americano / uma amiga americana.
3 Trabalho muito...
4 mas não tenho muito dinheiro.
5 Tenho dois filhos.
6 Os filhos têm seis e oito anos.
7 Infelizmente trabalho com um computador; é chato.
8 A minha esposa trabalha para uma companhia em Bath.
9 Tenho casa em Faro.
10 Tenho férias em Abril.

▶ Let's speak Portuguese – fast and fluently

No more stuttering and stumbling! Get out the stopwatch and time yourself with this fluency practice.

Translate each section and check if it is correct, then cover up the answers and say the three or four sentences fast!

20 seconds per section for a silver star, 15 seconds for a gold star.

Some of the English is in 'Portuguese-speak' to help you.

Good evening. I am going to Lisbon. You, too?
No, I work in Lisbon – in a (*num*) bank. Now I am going to Sintra.
I have holidays – without the computer.

Boa noite. Vou para Lisboa. O senhor / a senhora também?
Não, eu trabalho em Lisboa – num banco. Agora vou para Sintra.
Tenho férias – sem o computador.

How is Sintra? Is it big?
No, it is not big, but it is not boring.
It is very lovely and it costs a lot.
I have a girlfriend, (the) Lúcia.

Como é Sintra? É grande?
Não, não é grande, mas não é chata.
É muito bonita e custa muito.
Tenho uma amiga, a Lúcia.

She has a house in Sintra.
A hotel costs a lot of money.
Oh, excuse me. One moment, please, it is (the) Lúcia.
She is always on the phone. 'Bye!

Tem uma casa em Sintra.
Um hotel custa muito dinheiro.
Oh, desculpe. Um momento, se faz favor, é a Lúcia.
Está sempre ao telefone. Adeus!

Now say **all** the sentences in Portuguese without stopping and starting.

If you can do it in under one minute you are a fast and fluent winner!

But if you are not happy with your result – just try once more.

▶ Learn by heart

Don't be tempted to skip this exercise because it reminds you of school. If you want to speak, not stumble, saying a few lines by heart does the trick! Learn **Chamo-me...** by heart after you have filled in the gaps with your personal, or any, information.

When you know the lines by heart, go over them again until you can say them aloud fluently and fairly fast. Can you beat 40 seconds?

Chamo-me...

Chamo-me...(*name*).
Sou de ....(*place*).
Estive em/no..............................(*place*) em.................... (*month*).
Trabalhei três anos para o/a ....(*name of firm*).
Agora trabalho para o/a...(*name of firm*).
Tenho uma casa em ....(*place*) e custa muito dinheiro.
Em Agosto vamos para ....(*place*).
Como é Faro em Janeiro, bonito ou não?

Test your progress

This is your only written exercise. You'll be amazed at how easy it is! Translate the 20 sentences without looking at the previous pages. The bits in brackets show 'Portuguese-speak' to help you.

1 My name is Peter Smith.
2 Hello, I am Paulo and this is Helen.
3 I am from Lisbon. And you (Sir)?
4 (The) Maria is a good friend.
5 I always go home in June.
6 We work in (the) Estoril in August.
7 I worked in New York in March.
8 What is it that you do? Do you work in computing?
9 I was in London with the children.
10 One moment, please. What is it? Does it cost a lot?
11 Does the house have a telephone? No, unfortunately not.
12 Good day. Are you (the) Mr Soares from (the) Porto?
13 I worked for an American company.
14 Now I have a better job. I work for three big banks.
15 Luís! Are we going to Faro?
16 My wife is American too. She is from Boston.
17 We have good seats in the aeroplane.
18 Do I have a Mercedes? No, unfortunately not!
19 My (girl)friend works, but not a lot.
20 I am going on holiday with (the) Teresa. Unfortunately, she is boring.

When you have finished, look up the answers on page 86, and mark your work following the scoring instructions. Then enter your result on the **Progress chart** on page 9. If your score is higher than 80% you'll have done very well indeed!

02

week two

Thirty-five minutes a day – but a little extra will speed up your progress!

25

Day one

- Read **In Silves**.
- Listen to/Read **Em Silves**.
- Listen to/Read the **New words**. Learn 20 easy ones.

Day two

- Repeat **Em Silves** and the **New words**.
- Go over **Pronunciation**.
- Learn the harder **New words**.
- Cut out the **Flash words** and use them to help you.

Day three

- Learn all the **New words** until you know them well.
- Read and learn the **Good news grammar**.

Day four

- Cut out and learn the **Flash sentences**.
- Listen to/Read **Learn by heart**.

Day five

- Listen to/Read **Let's speak Portuguese**.
- Go over **Learn by heart**.

Day six

- Listen to/Read **Let's speak more Portuguese** (optional).
- Listen to/Read **Let's speak Portuguese – fast and fluently** (optional).
- Translate **Test your progress**.

Day seven is a study-free day!

In Silves

In Faro Tom and Kate hire a car and drive to Silves. They speak to Maria Fernandes of Casa Maria, and later to Luís, the waiter. (*The English of Weeks 1–3 is in 'Portuguese-speak' to get you tuned in.*)

Kate   Good afternoon. Have you a room double for one night and not very expensive, please?

Maria   Yes, I have a room small with bathroom, but the shower is broken. My husband can it repair tomorrow.

Tom   Right, where is the room?

Maria   Here on the left. Not it is very big.

Kate   The room is a little small but nice. How much costs it?

Maria   Only €35 but not we accept credit cards. There is a big breakfast from (the) eight to (the) ten and half.

Kate   All right, €35 with breakfast. But can we take the breakfast at (the) eight less a quarter? We would like to go to Lagos tomorrow at (the) eight and a quarter.

Maria   That's all right.

Kate   Can I you ask where we can take a coffee? Is there a cafeteria near from here or a bar? Where are they?

Maria   It is very easy. There is a cafeteria at five minutes from here, at some 30 metres to the right and then straight ahead.

(In the cafeteria)

Luís   What would you like to take, please?

Kate   We would like a coffee with milk and a tea, please.

Luís   And something to eat? We have sandwiches, cod cakes, shrimp rissoles…

Tom   Right… four rissoles, please.

Tom   The table not is clean.

Kate   Yes, but the coffee not is bad.

Tom   The tea is cold.

Kate   Yes, but the toilets are great.

Tom   The rissoles are bad.

Kate   Yes, but the waiter is very handsome.

Tom   I would like the bill, please.

Luís   €9.10, please.

▶ Em Silves

In Faro Tom and Kate hire a car and drive to Silves. They speak to Maria Fernandes of Casa Maria, and later to Luís, the waiter.

Kate   Boa tarde. Tem um quarto de casal para uma noite, e não muito caro, se faz favor?

Maria   Sim, tenho um quarto pequeno com casa de banho, mas o duche está avariado. O meu marido pode consertá-lo amanhã.

Tom   Bom, onde é o quarto?

Maria   Aqui, à esquerda. Não é muito grande.

Kate   O quarto é um pouco pequeno, mas bonito. Quanto custa?

Maria   Só trinta e cinco euros, mas não aceitamos cartões de crédito. Há pequeno almoço das oito até às dez e meia.

Kate   Está bem, trinta e cinco euros com pequeno almoço. Mas podemos tomar o pequeno almoço às oito menos um quarto? Queríamos ir para Lagos amanhã às oito e um quarto.

Maria   Está bem.

Kate   Posso lhe perguntar onde podemos tomar um café? Há um café perto daqui... ou um bar? Onde?

Maria   É muito fácil. Há um café a cinco minutos daqui, a uns trinta metros à direita e logo em frente.

(*No café*)

Luís   O que querem tomar, por favor?

Kate   Queríamos um café com leite e um chá, se faz favor.

Luís   E alguma coisa para comer? Temos sandes, pastéis de bacalhau, rissóis de camarão...

Tom   Bom... quatro rissóis, se faz favor.

Tom   A mesa não está limpa.

Kate   Sim, mas o café não é mau.

Tom   O chá está frio.

Kate   Sim, mas os lavabos são excelentes.

Tom   Os rissóis estão maus.

Kate   Sim, mas o empregado é muito bonito.

Tom   Queria a conta, se faz favor.

Luís   Nove euros e dez cêntimos, se faz favor.

▶ New words

um quarto de casal *a double room*
uma noite *a night*
muito *very*
caro/a *expensive*
pequeno/a *small*
a casa de banho *the bathroom*
o duche *the shower*
avariado/a *broken*
o meu marido *my husband*
o, a (by itself) *it*
pode *he/she/it can, you can*
consertar *(to) repair*
consertá-lo *to repair it*
amanhã *tomorrow*
bom (by itself) *(all) right, OK*
onde *where*
aqui *here*
à esquerda *on/to the left*
um pouco *a little, a bit*
quanto…? *how much…?*
só *only*
trinta e cinco *thirty-five*
os cartões de crédito *the credit cards*
há *there is, there are*
o pequeno almoço *the breakfast*
meia *half*
está bem *(all) right, OK*
podemos *we can, may*
tomar *(to) take, have*
menos *less*
um quarto *a quarter (also: a room)*
queria/queríamos *I/we would like (to)*
ir *(to) go*

posso *I can, may*
perguntar *(to) ask*
posso lhe perguntar? *can I ask you?*
o café *the coffee, café*
perto (daqui) *near (here)*
ou *or*
fácil *easy*
os minutos *the minutes*
uns/umas *some*
trinta metros *thirty metres*
à direita *on/to the right*
logo *then, later*
em frente (de) *straight ahead, in front (of)*
o que querem? *what do you want?*
o leite *the milk*
um chá *a tea*
alguma coisa *something*
comer *(to) eat*
a sandes *the sandwich*
os pastéis de bacalhau *the cod cakes*
os rissóis de camarão *the shrimp rissoles*
a mesa *the table*
limpo/a *clean*
mau/má *bad*
frio/a *cold*
os lavabos *the toilets*
estão *they are, you are*
excelente *great, marvellous*
o empregado *the waiter*
a conta *the bill*
o cêntimo *cent*

TOTAL NEW WORDS: 64
…only 252 words to go!

▶ Good news grammar

1 *Ser* and *estar*: to be and (not) to be

Unless you are a genius you are bound to get these two mixed up at times. But with **Instant Portuguese** everybody will still understand you perfectly. Here are the main differences between **ser** and **estar** which both mean *(to) be*.

You use **ser** when you talk about something which is a basic characteristic of somebody or something and which does not change:

> **Sou** Tom Walker.
> **Somos** de Manchester.
> O empregado é muito bonito.

You also use **ser** for telling the time:

> Qué horas **são**? É uma (hora).

You use **estar** when you talk about something that is temporary, that can change.

> As mesas não **estão** limpas. O cha **está** frio.

You also use **estar** when someone or something is temporarily in a place.

> Não **estamos** em Londres. Onde **está** (o senhor)?
> But: Lisboa é em Portugal.

And if you confuse them? No need to get red in the face. It's not that serious!

Here is a combined verb box. Spend five minutes on it.

ser *(to) be*		**estar** *(to) be*
sou... João	*I am*	estou... em Lagos
é	*you* (sing.) *are*	está
é	*he/she/it is*	está
somos	*we are*	estamos
são	*you* (pl.) *are*	estão
são	*they are*	estão

Remember, *you* and ... *you*: use é and **está** when you talk to one person. Use **são** and **estão** when you talk to two people or more.

2 Asking questions

É **bom**. *It is good*. É **bom?** *Is it good?* You simply use your voice to turn a statement into a question. Very easy!

3 Saying 'not'

If you want to say in Portuguese that you are *not* doing something, you just add **não**. But did you notice what happened to the **não** when Senhora Fernandes said: '**Não** é muito grande' and '**Não** aceitamos cartões de crédito'? The **não** moved in front of the verb. It does this all the time: '*...not it is very big*' '*...not we take credit cards*'.

*The table **not** is clean.*   A mesa **não** está limpa.
*I **not** do work.*   **Não** trabalho.

Não, não trabalho – don't let this confuse you. The first **não** means *no*, the second one *not*.

4 *Há*: there is/is there? – there are/are there?

You will use this a lot, especially when asking questions.

Há um banco perto daqui? Há um bar? Há lavabos?

5 Telling the time: say 'less a quarter', 'and a quarter', 'and half'

São sete **menos um quarto**.	*It's **a quarter to** seven.*
São dez e **um quarto**.	*It's **a quarter past** ten.*
São duas e **meia**.	*It's **half past** two.*
É uma e **meia**.	*It's **half past** one.*

▶ Learn by heart

Learn **Não tenho muito dinheiro, mas...** by heart.

When you know it, try to say it fluently and fairly fast. How about 45 to 60 seconds? Once again, give this piece some life and dramatize it. Bits of it will come in handy later!

Choose one of these to fill in the gap:
   o meu marido, a minha esposa, o meu amigo, a minha amiga

Não tenho muito dinheiro, mas...

Não tenho muito dinheiro, mas queria ir de férias em Julho.
Queria ir ao Algarve com o/a .... (*person*).
Podemos ir a Lagos no Rover.
Não custa muito dinheiro e o Algarve é muito bonito.
Podemos ir? Não!
Há sempre muito trabalho na companhia e ...
o Rover está avariado!

▶ Let's speak Portuguese

Now let's practise what you have learned. I'll give you ten English sentences and you say them in Portuguese – OUT LOUD! If you have the recording, listen to check your answers. If you don't have the recording, cover up the answers at the bottom of this page. Tick each sentence if you get it right. Unless you get all ten correct, do the exercise again.

1 Do you have a room?
2 It is a little big.
3 At what time is the breakfast?
4 The computers are expensive.
5 We would like to eat something.
6 How much is (costs) the tea?
7 Where is the café? On the right?
8 We are going to Albufeira at two.
9 Excuse me, the bill, please.
10 Is there a bank near here?

Now answer the questions on the left with **Sim,** and speak about yourself, and those on the right with **Não** and say 'we'.

11 Tem um cartão Visa?   14 Estão de férias?
12 Há um bar aqui?   15 Os senhores trabalham dez horas?
13 É uma conta muito grande? 16 Têm muito dinheiro?

Now think up your own answers. Yours may be different from mine but quite correct.

17 A que horas é que (o senhor/senhora) vai para Lisboa?
18 Como estão os pastéis?
19 Onde é a Casa Maria?
20 Há lavabos aqui? Onde são?

If you managed to get more than half right the first time, give yourself a double star!

Answers

1 Tem um quarto?
2 É um pouco grande.
3 A que horas é o pequeno almoço?
4 Os computadores são caros.
5 Queríamos comer alguma coisa.
6 Quanto custa o chá?
7 Onde é o café? À direita?
8 Vamos para Albufeira às duas.
9 Desculpe, a conta, se faz favor.
10 Há um banco perto daqui?

11 Sim, tenho um cartão Visa.
12 Sim, há um bar aqui.
13 Sim, é uma conta muito grande.
14 Não, não estamos de férias.
15 Não, não trabalhamos dez horas.
16 Não, não temos muito dinheiro.
17 Vou para Lisboa às três e meia.
18 Os pastéis estão bons.
19 A Casa Maria é em Silves.
20 Sim, há lavabos aqui. São em frente.

▶ Let's speak more Portuguese

Here are the two optional exercises. Remember, they may stretch the 35 minutes a day by 15 minutes. But the extra practice will be worth it.

In your own words

This exercise will teach you to express yourself freely.

Use only the words you have learned so far.

Ask me in your own words...

1 if there is availability of a double room en suite
2 what the price of the room is for one night
3 where you can have a coffee

Tell me...

4 that there is a café straight ahead, and then on the right
5 you would like (the) breakfast at 7.30
6 you are thinking of driving to Coimbra the next day
7 you want coffee and cakes
8 what you don't like about the café
9 what Kate likes about the café (*Diz* (she says):...)
10 that the bill is €9.10

Answers

1 Tem um quarto de casal com casa de banho ou com duche?
2 Quanto custa o quarto para uma noite?
3 Onde há um café perto daqui?
4 Há um café em frente, e logo à direita.
5 Queria o pequeno almoço às sete e meia.
6 Queria ir a Coimbra amanhã.
7 Queria café e pastéis.
8 A mesa não está limpa e os rissóis estão maus.
9 Kate diz: 'Os lavabos são excelentes e o empregado é muito bonito'.
10 A conta é nove euros e dez cêntimos.

▶ Let's speak Portuguese – fast and fluently

No more stuttering and stumbling! Get out the stopwatch and time yourself with this fluency practice.

Translate each section and check if it is correct, then cover up the answers and say the three or four sentences fast!

20 seconds per section for a silver star, 15 seconds for a gold star.

Some of the English is in 'Portuguese-speak' to help you.

Good evening, do you have a room with bath?
80 (oitenta) euros is a little expensive.
I would like a room with shower.
How much is (costs) the breakfast?

Boa noite. Tem um quarto com banho?
Oitenta euros é um pouco caro.
Queria um quarto com duche.
Quanto custa o pequeno almoço?

To go to my company? Straight ahead, then on the left.
But I am going tomorrow to Mafra.
I would like to go at 9.30.

Para ir à minha companhia? Em frente, depois à esquerda.
Mas vou amanhã a Mafra.
Queria ir às nove e meia.

The café here is very small and expensive.
The toilets are not clean.
The coffee is cold and there is no tea.
The bill? Two cakes – eight euros?

O café aqui é muito pequeno e caro.
Os lavabos não estão limpos.
O café está frio e não há chá.
A conta? Dois pastéis – oíto euros?

Now say **all** the sentences in Portuguese without stopping and starting.

If you can do it in under a minute you are a fast and fluent winner!

But if you are not happy with your result – just try once more.

Test your progress

Translate these sentences into Portuguese and write them down. See what you can remember without looking at the previous pages.

1 Where is there a telephone? On the right?
2 Can we eat some rissoles here? Are there seats for four?
3 Do you have a table? At half past eight? We are six.
4 Let's go to Lagos, all right?
5 Can you repair the Ford? It is broken.
6 We are in the room. Where are you?
7 The cod cakes are excellent. I can eat lots.
8 Can I ask you? You have a small company. Is it in Texas?
9 We cannot go on holiday in July. We do not have money.
10 Where is the waiter? Does he have my bill?
11 Where are the toilets? On the left?
12 (The) Maria and I would like to go to Évora – without husbands.
13 Excuse me, I have only €35 and a credit card.
14 €3.10 for a sandwich? It is very expensive.
15 I was in Loulé for (*por*) one night. It costs less in November.
16 (The) Manuela is very good-looking. Where does she work? Very near?
17 All right! We take (*tomamos*) four teas with milk, please.
18 London is not pretty in November.
19 I have worked a little with computers. It is not easy.
20 How many months have we been here? Ten?

Check your answers on page 87 and follow the scoring instructions. Then enter your result on the **Progress chart** on page 9.

Another 80% …?

03

week three

Study for 35 minutes a day – but there are no penalties for doing more!

Day one

- Read **Let's go shopping**.
- Listen to/Read **Vamos fazer compras**.
- Listen to/Read the **New words**, then learn some of them.

Day two

- Repeat **Vamos fazer compras** and the **New words**.
- Learn all the **New words**.
- Cut out the **Flash words** and use them to help you.

Day three

- Test yourself on all the **New words** – boring, boring, but you are over halfway already!
- Listen to/Read **Spot the keys**.
- Read and learn the **Good news grammar**.

Day four

- Go over the **Good news grammar**.
- Cut out and learn the ten **Flash sentences**.

Day five

- Listen to/Read **Let's speak Portuguese**.
- Listen to/Read **Learn by heart**.

Day six

- Listen to/Read **Let's speak more Portuguese** (optional).
- Listen to/Read **Let's speak Portuguese – fast and fluently** (optional).
- Go over **Learn by heart**.
- Have a quick look at the **New words** for Weeks 1–3.
- You now know over 228 words! Well, more or less.
- Translate **Test your progress**.

Day seven

Enjoy your day off!

day-by-day guide

Let's go shopping

Tom and Kate have rented a holiday apartment just outside Lagos. Kate plans to do some shopping. (*The English of Weeks 1–3 is in 'Portuguese-speak' to get you tuned in.*)

Kate   Today we must go and do (some) shopping. Are we going to the town centre?

Tom   But it makes bad weather. It makes cold and there is football and tennis in the television… and golf at (the) noon and half…

Kate   I am very sorry, but first we must go to a cashpoint and to a tobacconist or to the post office to buy stamps… and then to the chemist's and to the dry cleaner's.

Tom   Is that all? And so not there is golf… perhaps football at (the) three…

Kate   No. We must go to the shopping centre to buy a suitcase new, and I must go to a supermarket and to the hairdresser's. And then I would like to buy some shoes.

Tom   Good grief! (My God!) Until what hour stay open the shops?

Kate   I believe that until (the) eight.

Tom   And so not there is football… perhaps tennis at eight and a quarter…

(Later)

Kate   I believe that I have bought too much; half kilo of ham, half kilo of cheese, 200 grams of pâté, eggs, bread, butter, sugar, six beers and a bottle of wine dyed (red).

Tom   There is enough for two days. Not we have eaten anything since yesterday. And what is there in the bag big? Something for me?

Kate   Well, I went to the hairdresser's in the shopping centre and afterwards I saw some shoes blue. They are great, aren't they? The sales assistant was very nice and handsome like (the) Tom Cruise.

Tom   Who is (the) Tom Cruise? And how much did cost the shoes?

Kate   They were a little expensive… €100… It is the same price in (the) England.

Tom   The what? My wife is mad!

Kate   But this T-shirt of golf was very cheap, size 4, only €10, and here I have a newspaper English, and… not there is tennis in the television now?

▶ Vamos fazer compras

Tom and Kate have rented a holiday apartment just outside Lagos. Kate plans to do some shopping.

Kate   Hoje temos de ir fazer compras. Vamos ao centro da cidade?

Tom   Mas faz mau tempo. Faz frio, e há futebol e ténis na televisão... e golfe ao meio-dia e meia...

Kate   Sinto muito, mas primeiro temos de ir ao multibanco, e a uma tabacaria ou ao Correio para comprar selos... e depois à farmácia e à tinturaria.

Tom   Isso é tudo? Então, não há golfe... talvez futebol às três...

Kate   Não. Temos de ir ao centro comercial para comprar uma mala nova, e eu tenho de ir a um supermercado e ao cabeleireiro. E logo queria comprar uns sapatos.

Tom   Meu Deus! Até que horas ficam abertas as lojas?

Kate   Creio que até às oito.

Tom   Então, não há futebol... talvez ténis às oito e um quarto...

(Mais tarde)

Kate   Creio que comprei demasiado: meio quilo de fiambre, meio quilo de queijo, duzentos gramas de patê, ovos, pão, manteiga, açúcar, seis cervejas e uma garrafa de vinho tinto.

Tom   Há bastante para dois dias. Não comemos nada desde ontem. E o que há no saco grande? Alguma coisa para mim?

Kate   Pois, fui ao cabeleireiro no centro comercial e depois vi uns sapatos azuis. São magníficos, não são? O vendedor era muito amável e bonito, como o Tom Cruise.

Tom   Quem é o Tom Cruise? E quanto custaram os sapatos?

Kate   Eram um pouco caros... cem euros... É o mesmo preço na Inglaterra.

Tom   O quê? A minha esposa está louca!

Kate   Mas esta T-shirt de golfe foi muito barata, tamanho quatro, só dez euros, e aqui tenho um jornal inglês, e... não há ténis na televisão agora?

▶ New words

hoje   today
temos de   we have to, must
ir fazer compras   to go shopping
ao centro da cidade   to the town centre
faz mau tempo   it is bad weather (lit. it makes…)
faz frio   it is cold (lit. it makes cold)
o futebol   the football
o ténis   the tennis
o golfe   the golf
a televisão   the television
sinto muito   I'm very sorry
primeiro   first
o multibanco   a cashpoint
a tabacaria   the tobacconist
o Correio   the post office
comprar   (to) buy
os selos   the stamps
depois   afterwards, then
a farmácia   the chemist's
a tinturaria   the dry cleaner's
então   and so, well
talvez   perhaps
esse/essa/isso   (by itself) that
tudo   all
o centro comercial   the shopping centre
uma mala   a suitcase
novo/a   new
tenho de   I have to, must
um supermercado   a supermarket
o cabeleireiro   the hairdresser's
queria   I would like (to)
os sapatos   the shoes
até   until
ficam   they stay
aberto/a   open
a loja   the shop
creio   I believe
que   that

mais   more
mais tarde   later
comprei   I (have) bought
demasiado   too much
o quilo   the kilo
o fiambre   the ham
o queijo   the cheese
duzentos/as   two hundred
um grama   a gram
o patê   the pâté
os ovos   the eggs
o pão   the bread
a manteiga   the butter
o açúcar   the sugar
a cerveja   the beer
uma garrafa   a bottle
o vinho tinto   the red wine
bastante   enough (also: rather)
comemos   we ate/have eaten (also: we eat)
nada   nothing
desde   since
ontem   yesterday
o saco   the bag
para mim   for me
fui   I was/I went/have gone
vi   I saw/have seen
azuis (azul)   blue
magnífico/a   great
não são?   aren't they?
o vendedor   sales assistant
era/eram   I/he/she/it was/you/they were
amável   nice, kind
como   like
quem   who
custaram   they (have) cost
foi, foram   I/he/she/it was/went/you/they were/went
cem   a hundred
o mesmo   the same
o preço   the price

na Inglaterra	*in England*	**o tamanho**	*the size*
louco/a	*mad, crazy*	**um jornal**	*a newspaper*
este/esta	*this*	**inglês/a**	*English*
barato/a	*cheap*		

TOTAL NEW WORDS: 84
...only 168 words to go!

More easy extras

Cores (colours)

branco/a	*white*	**amarelo/a**	*yellow*
preto/a	*black*	**castanho/a**	*brown*
vermelho/a	*red*	**cinzento/a**	*grey*
azul	*blue*	**laranja**	*orange*
verde	*green*	**rosa**	*pink*

▶ Spot the keys

By now you can say many things in Portuguese. But what happens if you ask a question and do not understand the answer? Don't panic and go blank; just listen for the words you know. Any familiar words which you pick up will provide you with keywords – clues to what the other person is saying. If you have the recording, close the book now, listen to the dialogue and write down all the key words you have recognized.

Here's an example:

You **Desculpe, queria ir ao Correio. Onde é?**

Answer *Pois, é muito fácil:* siga **em frente até** *ao seguinte cruzamento com semáforos. Há alguns edifícios, entre eles* **uma casa vermelha à esquerda.** *Depois há um lar de reformados,* **e umas** *tantas* **lojas. À direita** *há* **uma tinturaria.** *Atravesse* **o centro comercial e** *verá* **o Correio.**

With a lot of words running into each other you still managed to pick up: **em frente – até – uma casa vermelha – à esquerda – umas lojas – à direita – tinturaria – o centro comercial – o Correio.** I think you'll get there!

▶ Good news grammar

1 The past

Imagine you are getting married today. You would say 'I do'. If it happened yesterday you would say 'I did'. When you talk about the past in Portuguese the same thing happens: the verb has to change. Let's use the example of **trabalhar** from Week 1. You learned the four verb forms **trabalho**, **trabalha**, **trabalhamos** and **trabalham** so you could tell who is working right now. But if you wanted to say that someone worked yesterday, last week or last year, those verb forms have to show it. To ease the mental acrobatics I have put them into neat pairs, first giving the present and then the past:

trabalh**o**	*I work*	trabalh**ei**	*I worked*
trabalh**a**	*you* (sing.) *work*	trabalh**ou**	*you* (sing.) *worked*
	he/she/it works		*he/she/it worked*
trabalh**amos**	*we work*	trabalh**ámos**	*we worked*
trabalh**am**	*you* (pl.) *work*	trabalh**aram**	*you* (pl.) *worked*
	they work		*they worked*

Did you spot the 'freebie': **trabalhámos**? No change except for the accent, which you don't hear. If you use any other regular verb ending in **-ar**, like **telefonar** or **comprar**, the endings are the same: **compro** – **comprei**: *I buy – I bought*.

Regular verbs ending in **-er** have a similar pattern but without the accent:

comer *(to) eat*				
Present	com**o**	com**e**	com**emos**	com**em**
Past	com**i**	com**eu**	com**emos**	com**eram**

Say both sets of verbs with your eyes closed until you know them well. Ten minutes each will do it.

2 *Vamos ao centro da cidade?*

a *to* and **o(s)** or **a(s)** *the* are always contracted to single words: **ao(s)**, **à(s)**. The same happens with **de** *of* and **em** *in*: **de + o(s) = do(s)**, **de + a(s) = da(s)**; **em + o(s) = no(s)**, **em + a(s) = na(s)**.

3 *Ter de*: must, have to

How often do you say: 'I have to' or 'I must'?

Tenho de trabalhar. Temos de comprar. Tem de ir?

Just don't forget the **de**!

▶ Let's speak Portuguese

Say the sentences one at a time – OUT LOUD – in your best Portuguese. If you have the recording, listen to check your answers. If not, cover up the answers below.

1 I am very sorry, I have to go.
2 We would like to go shopping.
3 Where are the shops?
4 At what time are they open?
5 I would like to buy bread.
6 Today it is very cold.
7 Good grief! That's too expensive.
8 We have to buy milk.
9 We ate at the commercial centre.
10 You don't have a TV?

Answer these questions using the 'I' form of the verb and the words in brackets.

11 O que comprou? (um jornal inglês)
12 Onde comprou isto? (no supermercado)
13 O que viu? (muitas lojas)
14 O que comeu? (bacalhau)
15 Quantas horas trabalhou? (oito horas)

Now answer these questions with **Não** and the 'we' form of the verb.

16 Telefonaram para a Inglaterra?
17 Compraram a televisão?
18 Têm de ir ao Correio?
19 Trabalharam no centro comercial?

Finally, make up a giant sentence without drawing breath using

20 agora – temos de ir – centro – a minha amiga – comprar – sapatos – o meu marido. *Start with:* **Agora...**

Answers

1 Desculpe, tenho de ir.
2 Queríamos ir fazer compras.
3 Onde são as lojas?
4 A que horas estão abertas?
5 Queria comprar pão.
6 Hoje faz muito frio.
7 Meu Deus! Isso é demasiado caro.
8 Temos de comprar leite.
9 Comemos no centro comercial.
10 Não tem televisão?
11 Comprei um jornal inglês.
12 Comprei isto no supermercado.
13 Vi muitas lojas.
14 Comi bacalhau.
15 Trabalhei oito horas.
16 Não, não telefonámos para a Inglaterra.
17 Não, não comprámos a televisão.
18 Não, não temos de ir ao Correio.
19 Não, não trabalhámos no centro comercial.
20 Agora temos de ir ao centro com a minha amiga para comprar sapatos para o meu marido.

▶ Let's speak more Portuguese

For these optional exercises add an extra 15 minutes to your daily schedule. And remember, don't worry about getting the article or endings wrong. Near enough is good enough!

In your own words

This exercise will teach you to express yourself freely. Use only the words you have learned so far.

Tell me in your own words that...

1 you would like to do the shopping today
2 you are aiming for the middle of the town
3 you are out of cash
4 you have to go first to an ATM...
5 then you have to go to the pharmacy
6 you have seen a shoe shop
7 you have to buy new shoes
8 you bought cheap shoes
9 you did not get much in the supermarket
10 you bought bread and butter, and white wine – ten bottles...

Answers
1 Queria ir fazer compras hoje.
2 Vou ao centro.
3 Não tenho dinheiro.
4 Primeiro tenho de ir a um multibanco.
5 Depois tenho de ir à farmácia.
6 Vi uma loja de sapatos.
7 Tenho de comprar sapatos novos.
8 Comprei sapatos baratos.
9 Não comprei muito no supermercado.
10 Comprei pão e manteiga e vinho branco – dez garrafas.

▶ Let's speak Portuguese – fast and fluently

Translate each section and check if it is correct, then cover up the answers and say the three or four sentences fast!

20 seconds per section for a silver star, 15 seconds for a gold star.

Some of the English is in 'Portuguese-speak' to help you.

Excuse me, are you going to buy a mobile phone?
Is it expensive, the blue mobile phone?
No, not much, in (the) England it is the same price.

Desculpe, vai comprar um telemóvel?
É caro o telemóvel azul?
Não, não muito, na Inglaterra é o mesmo preço.

I would like to buy a suitcase, but not very expensive.
We have a suitcase, but it is too small.
I have seen a suitcase, and it is rather big.

Queria comprar uma mala, mas não muito cara.
Temos uma mala, mas é demasiado pequena.
Vi uma mala, e é bastante grande.

The weather is very bad in April.
I went to Lisbon. I ate in the Baixa.
Ham, cheese and bread – the bill was 10 euros.
The waiter wasn't handsome but he was very nice.

Faz mau tempo em Abril.
Fui a Lisboa. Comi na Baixa.
Fiambre, queijo e pão – a conta foi dez euros.
O empregado não era bonito mas era muito amável.

Now say **all** the sentences in Portuguese without stopping and starting.

If you can do it in under one minute you are a fast and fluent winner!

But if you are not happy with your result – just try once more.

▶ Learn by heart

Once you have learned this dialogue, try to say it in under one minute!

Vamos fazer compras
A Hoje temos de ir fazer compras – vamos ao centro.
B Mas faz frio…
…
B Meu Deus! Não tenho dinheiro. Onde há um multibanco?
A Creio que comprei demasiado: pão, manteiga, fiambre e queijo… e seis garrafas de vinho branco.
B E as cervejas?
A Ah – desculpe!

Test your progress

Translate in writing – no looking back at the pages, mind. Then check the answers on page 88 and be amazed!

1 We can buy stamps at (in) the tobacconist's?
2 Did you work at the hairdresser's? No, at the chemist's.
3 (The) Maria was very kind, like always.
4 Good grief! All the cashpoints are broken!
5 Today is a rather good day.
6 The English newspaper is not cheap.
7 I believe that I saw a dry cleaner's in the commercial centre.
8 Until what time do you have to work? Until eight?
9 When do we have to go? I cannot go until later.
10 In November it is (makes) always bad weather in Manchester.
11 What did you buy? Six bottles of red wine? Great!
12 Size 4: what is that in English?
13 It is very cold in this (*nesta*) house. I must buy something.
14 First I went shopping and then we ate with friends.
15 Yesterday we bought a new TV. And today it is broken.
16 You bought a black case, not red.
17 Everything was very expensive, so we did not buy anything.
18 Who is the sales assistant? Where is there milk?
19 We do not have the T-shirt in green and at the same price. I am very sorry.
20 I would like to buy something. Something for me, but not very expensive.

Remember to fill in Week 3 on the **Progress chart**. You are now halfway home!

04

week four

Study for 35 minutes a day but if you are keen, try 40… 45…!

Day one

- Read **Let's go and eat**.
- Listen to/Read **Vamos comer**.
- Listen to/Read the **New words**. Learn the easy ones.

Day two

- Repeat the dialogue. Learn the harder **New words**.
- Cut out the **Flash words** and use them to help you.

Day three

- Learn all the **New words** until you know them well.
- Read and learn the **Good news grammar**.

Day four

- Listen to/Read **Learn by heart**.
- Cut out and learn the **Flash sentences**.

Day five

- Read **Say it simply**.
- Listen to/Read **Let's speak Portuguese**.

Day six

- Listen to/Read **Let's speak more Portuguese** (optional).
- Listen to/Read **Let's speak Portuguese – fast and fluently** (optional).
- Listen to/Read **Spot the keys**.
- Translate **Test your progress**.

Day seven

Are you keeping your scores above 60%? In that case… have a good day off!

day-by-day guide

Let's go and eat

Tom and Kate are still in Lagos. João Gomes invites them to dinner, where Luís, the head waiter, explains the menu.

Kate Tom, somebody from Lisbon telephoned. He didn't say why. I don't have the number – that's because at this moment I don't have paper. A name like Goles or Gomes.

Tom Ah yes, João Gomes, a good client of the company. I know him well. He is very nice. I have an appointment arranged with him on Tuesday. This is an important matter.

Tom (*On the phone*) Hello, good day, Mr Gomes! I am Tom Walker... Yes, thank you very much... yes, sure, that is possible... on Tuesday, next week... correct... that's all right... yes, very interesting... no, we don't have time... great... no, only a few days... oh, yes... when?... at nine... upstairs, at the exit... in front of the door. Well, until tonight, thank you very much, until later.

Kate What are we going to do tonight?

Tom We are going to eat with Mr Gomes, in the centre, behind the church. He says that the restaurant is new and very good. He is in Lagos for two days with Edith Palmer from our company.

Kate I know Edith Palmer. I do not like her. She is boring and very snobbish. She has a terrible dog. I believe that tonight I am going to be sick. A cold with pains. The doctor must come.

Tom No, please! Mr Gomes is an important client. One cannot do that!

(*In the restaurant*)

Luís There is no fish on the menu, and the dessert today is ice-cream of the house.

João Madam, what do you like? Perhaps a soup and then meat?

Kate A steak with salad, please.

Edith It is not good to eat too much red meat, Kate.

João Mr Walker, do you like lamb? And what would you like to drink?

⊷⊷⟶ Page 52

▶ Vamos comer

Tom and Kate are still in Lagos. João Gomes invites them to dinner, where Luís, the head waiter, explains the menu.

Kate   Tom, telefonou alguém de Lisboa. Não disse porquê. Não tenho o número – é que neste momento não tenho papel. Um nome como Goles, ou Gomes.

Tom   Ah, sim, João Gomes, um bom cliente da companhia. Conheço-o bem. É muito amável. Tenho um encontro marcado com ele na terça-feira. Isto é uma coisa importante.

Tom   *(Ao telefone)* Olá, bom dia, senhor Gomes! Sou o Tom Walker... Sim, muito obrigado... sim, certamente, isso é possível... na terça-feira, na semana que vem... exacto... está bem... sim, muito interessante... não, não temos tempo... excelente... não, só uns dias... ah, sim... quando?... às nove... em cima, à saída... em frente da porta. Então, até esta noite, muito obrigado, até logo.

Kate   O que vamos fazer esta noite?

Tom   Vamos jantar com o senhor Gomes, no centro, atrás da igreja. Diz que o restaurante é novo e muito bom. Ele está em Lagos por dois dias, com a Edith Palmer da nossa companhia.

Kate   Conheço a Edith Palmer. Não gosto dela. É chata e muito snob. Tem um cão terrível. Creio que esta noite vou estar doente. Uma constipação e dores. O médico tem de vir.

Tom   Não, por favor! O senhor Gomes é um cliente importante. Isso não se pode fazer!

(No restaurante)

Luís   Não há peixe na ementa, e a sobremesa hoje é gelado da casa.

João   A senhora, de que gosta? Talvez uma sopa e depois, carne?

Kate   Pois, um bife com salada, por favor.

Edith   Não é bom comer demasiada carne vermelha, Kate.

João   Senhor Walker, gosta de borrego? E o que quer beber?

⋯⋯➤ Page 53

Tom	Right, for me, lamb chops with chips and vegetables – but everything without garlic – and a beer, please.
Edith	Tom, garlic is good (for you). I like (it) very much.
João	And you?
Edith	The grilled chicken and a glass of still water, please.
(Later)	
João	Have we finished? Does anyone want dessert... fruit... a coffee? Nobody? Well then, the bill, please.
João	Ah, Senhor Gomes, could you help me, please? How do you say 'doggy bag' in Portuguese? I would like a bag for my dog.
Kate	But Edith, the dog is in England!

▶ New words

comer *(to) eat*
telefonou *(has) called, telephoned*
alguém *someone*
disse *(has) said*
é que *it is that, that's because...*
o papel *the paper*
um nome *a name*
um cliente *a client*
conheço *I know (somebody/place)*
bem *well, all right*
um encontro *an appointment*
marcado/a *arranged*
ele *him (also: he)*
a terça-feira *Tuesday*
uma coisa *a thing, matter*
importante *important*
(muito) obrigado/a *thank you (very much)*
certamente *sure, certainly*
possível *possible*
na semana que vem *next week*
exacto *correct, exactly*
interessante *interesting*
o tempo *time (also: weather)*
em cima *above, upstairs*
a saída *the exit*

a porta *the door*
vamos fazer *we are going to do*
jantar *to dine*
atrás (de) *behind*
a igreja *the church*
diz *he/she/it says, you say*
o restaurante *the restaurant*
durante *during*
o(s) nosso(s)/a(s) nossa(s) *our*
(não) gosto de *I (do not) like*
snob *snobbish*
um cão *a dog*
terrível *terrible, awful*
doente *sick, ill*
uma constipação *a cold*
a dor *pain*
o médico *the doctor*
vir *(to) come*
isso não se pode fazer *one cannot do that*
o peixe *the fish*
a ementa *the menu*
a sobremesa *the dessert*
o gelado *the ice-cream*
gosta (de)? *do you like?*
uma sopa *a soup*
a carne *the meat*
um bife *a steak*
uma salada *a salad*

Tom	Bom, para mim, costeletas de borrego com batatas fritas e legumes – mas tudo sem alho – e uma cerveja, por favor.
Edith	Tom, o alho faz muito bem. Eu gosto muito.
João	E a senhora?
Edith	O frango grelhado e um copo de água sem gás, por favor.

(Mais tarde)

João	Já terminámos? Alguém quer sobremesa... fruta... um café? Ninguém? Bom, a conta, se faz favor.
Edith	Ah, senhor Gomes, podia-me ajudar, por favor? Como se diz 'doggy bag' em português? Queria um saco para o meu cão.
Kate	Mas Edith, o cão está na Inglaterra!

o borrego   *the lamb*
o que quer?   *what do you want?*
beber   *(to) drink*
as costeletas   *the chops*
as batatas fritas   *the chips*
os legumes   *the vegetables*
o alho   *the garlic*
o frango grelhado   *the grilled chicken*
a fruta   *the fruit*
um copo   *a glass*

a água   *the water*
com/sem gás   *fizzy/still*
já terminámos?   *have we finished?*
ninguém   *nobody*
podia-me ajudar?   *could you help me?*
como...?   *how...?*
Como se diz ... em português?   *How does one say ... in Portuguese?*
um saco   *a bag*

TOTAL NEW WORDS: 71
...only 97 words to go!

Last easy extras

Os dias da semana (the days of the week)

a segunda-feira	*Monday*	**a sexta-feira**	*Friday*
a terça-feira	*Tuesday*	**o sábado**	*Saturday*
a quarta-feira	*Wednesday*	**o domingo**	*Sunday*
a quinta-feira	*Thursday*		

If you are obviously talking about the days of the week, you can drop the final -feira.

More numbers

11	onze	19	dezanove	50	cinquenta
12	doze	20	vinte	60	sessenta
13	treze	21	vinte e um/uma	70	setenta
14	catorze	22	vinte e dois/duas	80	oitenta
15	quinze	23	vinte e três, *etc.*	90	noventa
16	dezasseis	30	trinta	100	cem (cento)
17	dezassete	31	trinta e um/uma, *etc.*	200	duzentos/as
18	dezoito	40	quarenta	1,000	mil

More about time

Que horas são?	*What is the time?*	uma hora	*an hour*
A que horas?	*At what time?*	um dia	*a day*
às cinco	*at five o'clock*	uma semana	*a week*
É à uma.	*It is at one o'clock.*	um mês	*a month*
È às duas.	*It is at two o'clock.*	um ano	*a year*
um minuto	*a minute*		

▶ Good news grammar

1 The future

There is an easy way to say something is going to happen in the future. You don't use *shall* or *will* but simply: *going to* or *go to.*

Vamos comprar pão.   *We are going to buy bread.*

2 *Gosto de – não gosto de – gosta de?* I like – I don't like – do you like?

You'll use this a lot. Remember to slip in the **de!**

De que **gosta** (o/a senhor/a)?   *What do you like?*
Gosto de fazer compras.   *I like to shop.*
Não **gostamos da** Edith.   *We don't like Edith.*

3 A verb a day... the first six

Unfortunately, even with all the shortcuts, you can't speak Portuguese without verbs. And worse, there's no magic wand for knowing verbs and verb forms without a bit of old-fashioned drill.

But the good news is that the more verbs you know, the more you can say. And with each verb it gets easier.

Most regular -ar and -er verbs have the familiar pattern of **trabalhar** and **comer**, so know one – know lots more. But there are also odd ones out – with irregular endings which wreck the rules just when you think you know them!

This week learn a verb a day, both in the present and the past tense.

Over the next six days learn **crer** to believe, **dizer** to say, **fazer** to do, **ir** to go, **poder** can and **ver** to see. Spend 15 minutes on each one. You'll find the verbs in Week 6 on page 79. The present tense is printed in straight letters and the past tense underneath is in italics.

▶ Learn by heart

Here is someone who is rather fed up. Act out the dialogue in 45 seconds!

Não gosto...

A Conhece o senhor Gomes? É um bom cliente da companhia. Tenho de ir jantar com ele.

B Ah, sim?

A Não gosto dele. Não é amável. Come muito e bebe demasiado.

B E quando vai jantar com ele?

A Esta noite! Há futebol na televisão. Queria ter uma constipação mas isso não se pode fazer. Sempre a companhia...!

B Sinto muito.

Say it simply

When people want to speak Portuguese but don't dare, it's usually because they are trying to translate what they want to say from English into Portuguese. And when they don't know some of the words, they give up.

With **Instant Portuguese** you work around the words you don't know with the words you do know.

Believe me, with about 400 words you can say anything.

It may not always be very elegant, but you are communicating!

Here are two examples showing you how to say things in a simple way. Words that are not part of the **Instant** vocabulary have been highlighted.

1 You **need** to **change** your **flight** from Tuesday to Friday. Saying it simply:

Não podemos ir na terça-feira, queríamos ir na sexta.

Or: **Não é possível ir na terça-feira, temos de ir na sexta.**

2 You are on a city tour and have just realized that you **left** your **purse** in the restaurant. Saying it simply:

Sinto muito, tenho de ir ao restaurante. O meu dinheiro está no restaurante.

Or: **Tenho de ter o meu dinheiro. Infelizmente tudo está no restaurante.**

▶ Let's speak Portuguese

Here are ten sentences as a warm-up! Translate the English below and use the recording to check your answers if you have it.

1 I do not like the client.
2 Do we have to go with him?
3 What do you want, the meat or the fish?
4 Yes, sure, I would like to go.
5 Do you have an appointment for me?
6 I like going to Madeira.
7 Who did that?
8 Did someone call?
9 I know a cheap restaurant.
10 Could you help me, please?

Now pretend you are in Portugal with friends who do not speak Portuguese. They want you to ask someone things in Portuguese. They say, 'Please ask him...'

11 if he knows Edith Palmer.
12 if he likes lamb.
13 what he wants to drink.
14 if he has time next week.
15 if he has a dog.

On another occasion they ask you to tell someone things. In the first three examples they use words you don't know, so you have to use your **Instant** words. They say, 'Please tell her...'

16 the soup is stone cold.
17 that he/she is a vegetarian.
18 that we are in a rush now.
19 that nobody has seen John.
20 that he/she cannot go tomorrow.

Answers

1 Não gosto do cliente.
2 Temos de ir com ele?
3 O que quer, a carne ou o peixe?
4 Sim, certamente, queria ir.
5 Tem um encontro marcado para mim?
6 Gosto de ir à Madeira.
7 Quem fez isso?
8 Alguém telefonou?
9 Conheço um restaurante barato.
10 Podia ajudar-me, por favor?

11 Conhece Edith Palmer?
12 Gosta de borrego?
13 O que quer beber?
14 Tem tempo na semana que vem?
15 Tem cão?
16 A sopa está muito fria.
17 Ele/ela não come carne.
18 Desculpe, mas não temos tempo agora.
19 Ninguém viu o João.
20 Ele/ela não pode ir amanhã.

▶ Let's speak more Portuguese

In your own words

This exercise will teach you to express yourself freely. Use only the words you have learned so far.

Tell me in your own words that...

1 somebody has the number of (the) Carlos Lopes
2 you have an appointment arranged with him next week
3 he knows the company well
4 he is a very good and very important client
5 you are going to dine with (the) Carlos on (the) Thursday
6 (the) Edith Palmer cannot make it – she is ill
7 she doesn't have much time to go to the doctor, only two hours
8 you are very fond of lamb and garlic
9 nobody is eating fruit or cheese
10 they went to the restaurant at half past eleven

Answers

1 Alguém tem o número do Carlos Lopes.
2 Tenho um encontro marcado com ele na semana que vem.
3 Conhece bem a companhia.
4 É um cliente muito bom e muito importante.
5 Vou jantar com o Carlos na quinta(-feira).
6 A Edith Palmer não pode ir – está doente.
7 Não tem muito tempo para ir ao médico, só duas horas.
8 Gosto muito de borrego e de alho.
9 Ninguém come fruta ou queijo.
10 Foram ao restaurante às onze e meia.

▶ Let's speak Portuguese – fast and fluently

Translate each section and check if it is correct, then cover up the answers and say the three or four sentences fast!

20 seconds per section for a silver star, 15 seconds for a gold star.

Some of the English is in 'Portuguese-speak' to help you.

Do you know (the) Carlos Lopes? He phoned today.
Why? He said it was important.
The appointment was (foi) arranged for (the) Wednesday.

Conhece o Carlos Lopes? Telefonou hoje.
Porque? Disse que era importante.
O encontro foi marcado para a quarta(-feira).

Carlos is in Lisbon only until (the) Friday.
There is a new restaurant near the bank.
But I would like to eat with him at my house tonight.

O Carlos está em Lisboa só até a sexta(-feira).
Há um restaurante novo perto do banco.
Mas queria comer com ele na minha casa esta noite.

Unfortunately, I cannot go.
My dog is ill. He has pains. He has eaten too much meat.
Oh, I am very sorry. How do you say in Portuguese: 'Poor little thing?' ('Coitado.')

Infelizmente, não posso ir.
O meu cão está doente. Tem dores. Comeu demasiada carne.
Oh, sinto muito. Como se diz em português: 'Poor little thing'? 'Coitado.'

Now say **all** the sentences in Portuguese without stopping and starting.

If you can do it in under one minute you are a fast and fluent winner!

But if you are not happy with your result – just try once more.

▶ Spot the keys

You practised listening for key words when you asked the way to the post office in Week 3. Now you are in a department store and you ask the sales assistant if the black shoes you liked are also available in size 39:

Desculpe, tem estes sapatos também no número trinta e nove?

She said **não** then **um momento, se faz favor** and disappeared. When she came back, this is what she said:

Acabo de procurar no armazém e telefonei a outra loja, **mas só têm os sapatos em castanho**. *Mas sei por experiência que esta marca* **sempre vêm em tamanhos muito grandes** *e na minha opinião o* **número trinta e oito** *seria* **bastante grande**.

Size 39 was only available in brown, but size 38 might fit.

Test your progress

Write the Portuguese translations without looking at the previous pages.

1 What did he say? He said, 'For whom are the chips?'
2 Can you come to our house? Next week?
3 She says that the exit of the shop is upstairs behind the bar.
4 Did he say that he went to (the) England?
5 What do you want? It is that I am sick and I cannot work.
6 Could you help me, please? Is there a doctor here?
7 He is going to the arranged appointment without shoes? One cannot do that.
8 I know Lucia Pereira. She is a very interesting lady.
9 Nobody can drink 15 beers in one night. It is not possible.
10 I like the dessert very much. I would like the ice-cream.
11 I believe that it is an important matter, but we do not have time.
12 We have finished and now we must go to Braga.
13 I eat a lot of salads. What do you eat?
14 How do you like the fish? Without garlic?
15 The name of this vegetable: how does one say (it) in Portuguese?
16 There are no shops in front of the church or behind. What are we going to do?
17 The company phoned. A Mr Lopes said that it was not important.
18 Sure, they have fizzy water. They always have (it).
19 He says that he has pains since yesterday.
20 I have a cold. I cannot go to (the) England today.

How are your 'shares' looking on the **Progress chart**? Going up?

05

week five

How about 15 minutes on the train, tube or bus, 10 minutes on the way home and 30 minutes before switching on the television...?

Day one

- Read **On the move**.
- Listen to/Read **De cá para lá**.
- Read the **New words**. Learn 15 or more.

Day two

- Repeat the dialogue. Learn the harder **New words**.
- Cut out the **Flash words** to get stuck in.

Day three

- Test yourself to perfection on all the **New words**.
- Read and learn the **Good news grammar**.

Day four

- Listen to/Read **Learn by heart**.
- Cut out and learn the **Flash sentences**.

Day five

- Listen to/Read **Let's speak Portuguese**.
- Go over **Learn by heart**.

Day six

- Listen to/Read **Let's speak more Portuguese** (optional).
- Listen to/Read **Let's speak Portuguese – fast and fluently** (optional).
- Listen to/Read **Spot the keys**.
- Translate **Test your progress**.

Day seven

How is the **Progress chart** looking? Great? Great! I bet you don't want a day off... but I insist!

day-by-day guide

On the move

Tom and Kate are now travelling through the Algarve by train, bus and hire car. They talk to Ana, the ticket clerk at the station, to Jim on the train and later to Jorge, the bus driver.

(At the railway station)

Tom	Two tickets to Albufeira, please.
Ana	Thereandback?
Tom	There and what? Please speak more slowly.
Ana	There – and – back?
Tom	Single, please. When is there a train for Albufeira and on what platform?
Ana	At a quarter to ten, on platform number six.

(On the train)

Kate	Come on, Tom, there are two seats here in the non-smoking carriage. Oh, there is somebody here who is smoking. Excuse me, it is forbidden to smoke here.
Jim	Sorry, I don't understand, I speak only English.

(At the bus stop)

Kate	They say that the bus for Tavira is coming in some 20 minutes. Tom, please, here are my postcards and a letter. There is a post box down there. I am going to take some photos of the river. It is very lovely with the sun.
Tom	Kate, come on, two buses are coming. The two are yellow. This one is full. Let's take the other one.

(In the bus) Two to Tavira, please.

Jorge	This bus goes to Albufeira.
Tom	But we are in Albufeira!
Jorge	Yes, yes, but this bus goes up to the Albufeira hospital.

(In the hire car)

Tom	Here comes our car. It costs only €40 for three days. I am very pleased.
Kate	I do not like the car. I believe that it is very cheap because it is very old. Let's hope not to have problems...
Tom	I am very sorry, but the first car was too expensive, the second one too big, this one was the last.

····➡ Page 66

▶ De cá para lá

Tom and Kate are now travelling through the Algarve by train, bus and hire car. They talk to Ana, the ticket clerk at the station, to Jim on the train and later to Jorge, the bus driver.

(Na estação de caminho de ferro)

Tom Dois bilhetes para Albufeira se faz favor.

Ana Deidaevolta?

Tom De ida e quê? Fale mais devagar, se faz favor.

Ana De – ida – e – volta?

Tom Só ida, se faz favor. A que horas há um comboio para Albufeira, e em que linha?

Ana Às dez menos um quarto, na linha número seis.

(No comboio)

Kate Anda, vem, Tom, há dois lugares aqui na carruagem para não fumadores. Oh, aqui há alguém que está a fumar. Desculpe, é proibido fumar aqui.

Jim Sorry, não compreendo. Falo only English.

(Na paragem de autocarros)

Kate Dizem que o autocarro para Tavira vem dentro de uns vinte minutos. Tom, faz favor, aqui estão os meus postais e uma carta. Ali em baixo há um marco. Vou tirar umas fotos do rio. Está muito bonito com o sol.

Tom Kate, anda, vêm dois autocarros. Os dois são amarelos. Este está cheio. Vamos apanhar o outro.

(No autocarro) Dois para Tavira, se faz favor.

Jorge Este autocarro vai para Albufeira.

Tom Mas estamos em Albufeira!

Jorge Sim, sim, mas este autocarro vai até ao hospital de Albufeira.

(No carro de aluguer)

Tom Aqui vem o nosso carro. Custa só quarenta euros por três dias. Estou muito contente.

Kate Não gosto do carro. Creio que é muito barato porque é muito velho. Esperamos não ter problemas…

Tom Sinto muito, mas o primeiro carro era demasiado caro, o segundo demasiado grande, este era o último.

···■▶ Page 67

(Later)

There is no map. In which street are we? Where is the motorway? On the left there is a petrol station and a bus stop and on the right there is a school. Come on!

Kate The main road is over there, by the traffic lights. We go up to the end of the street, we arrive at the motorway. Perhaps some three kilometres.

(On the motorway)

Why does the car go very slowly? Do we have enough petrol? How many litres? Do we have oil? Is the engine hot? I believe the car has broken down. Where is the mobile? Where is the number of the garage? Where is my handbag?

Tom Kate, please, all this is giving me a headache! And here comes the rain. And why are the police driving behind us?

▶ New words

de cá para lá *from here to there*
a estação *the station*
o caminho de ferro *the railway*
o bilhete *the ticket*
ida e volta *return ticket (going and returning)*
fale *speak*
mais devagar *speak more slowly*
o comboio *the train*
a linha *the platform (lit. line, track)*
anda, vem! *come!, come on!*
a carruagem *the carriage*
não fumadores *non-smoking*
está a fumar *he/she is smoking*
proibido *forbidden*
fumar *(to) smoke*
compreendo *I understand*
falo *I speak*
a paragem *the stop*
o autocarro *the bus*
dizem *they say*
vem *he/she/it comes, you come*

os postais *the postcards*
a carta *the letter*
ali *there*
em baixo *below (also: downstairs)*
o marco *the post box*
tirar *(to) take, photograph*
a foto(grafia) *the photo(graph)*
o rio *the river*
o sol *the sun*
vêm *they come, are coming*
este *this*
cheio/a *full*
apanhar *to catch*
o/a outro/a *the other*
até *as far as (also: until)*
o hospital *the hospital*
o carro de aluguer *the hire car*
contente *happy, content*
porque *because*
velho/a *old*
esperamos *we hope, let's hope*
o problema *the problem*
o/a segundo/a *the second*
o/a último/a *the last*
o mapa *the map*

(Mais tarde)

Não há mapa. Em que rua estamos? Onde é a autoestrada? À esquerda há uma bomba de gasolina e uma paragem de autocarros e à direita há uma escola. Anda, vem!

Kate   A estrada é ali, aos sinais. Vamos até ao fim da rua, chegamos à autoestrada. Talvez uns três quilómetros.

(Na autoestrada)

Porque é que o carro vai muito devagar? Temos gasolina suficiente? Quantos litros? Temos óleo? O motor está quente? Creio que o carro está avariado. Onde está o telemóvel? Onde está o número da garagem? Onde está a minha bolsa?

Tom   Kate, por favor, tudo isto dá-me uma dor de cabeça. E aqui vem a chuva! E porque é que a polícia vem atrás de nós?

a rua *the street*
a autoestrada *the motorway*
a bomba de gasolina *the petrol station*
uma escola *a school*
a estrada *the main road*
os sinais *the traffic lights*
o fim *the end*
chegamos *we arrive*
o quilómetro *the kilometre*
porque...? *why...?*
suficiente *enough*
a gasolina *the petrol*

o litro *the litre*
o óleo *the oil*
o motor *the motor*
quente *hot*
a garagem *the garage*
o(s) meu(s)/a(s) minha(s) *my*
a bolsa *the handbag*
me *me*
dá *he/she/it gives, you give*
uma dor de cabeça *a headache*
a chuva *the rain*
a polícia *the police*

**TOTAL NEW WORDS: 70
...only 27 words to go!**

▶ Good news grammar

1 'It': *o* and *a* – 'them': *os* and *as*

If you want to refer to something or someone – o bilhete, a gasolina, os postais or as fotografias – in English, you would say 'it' or 'them'. In positive sentences in Portuguese you use o, a, os or as and attach it with a hyphen after the verb.

Compro o bilhete. Compro-o. Compro a gasolina. Compro-a. Compro os postais. Compro-os.

In negative sentences, o, a, etc. go before the verb and there isn't a hyphen. Não compro as fotografias. Não as compro.

The o, a etc. sometimes change to lo, la, los or las or even to no, na, nos or nas. But don't worry about it.

2 Pronouns: *me, mim, o, a, ele, ela; nos, os, as* etc.

Learning these 'cold' is rather disagreeable. Pick them up from the dialogues or from the **Flash sentences**. It's easier that way.

3 A verb a day... the last six

Here are the last six verbs which need the daily drill: **dar** *to give*, **querer** *to want, wish*, **saber** *to know*, **vir** *to come*, **ser** *to be* and **estar** *to be*. Pick one for each day and spend ten minutes memorizing both the present and past tense from the verb list on page 79. **Ser** and **estar** are old friends from Week 1, so you only have to learn the missing bits. The rest of the 30 **Instant** verbs have the same endings as **trabalhar** and **comer**. Know these two – know the rest!

▶ Learn by heart

Someone has crashed the car and someone else is getting suspicious. Say these lines like a prize-winning play!

Vamos ao ténis

A Vamos ao ténis? Tenho dois bilhetes da companhia. Gosto muito dos americanos. Vamos de autocarro ou talvez de metro. Há também um comboio, todo o dia.

B O autocarro, o metro, um comboio? Porque? Há uma coisa de que não gosto. Temos um carro em baixo na rua.

A Com a chuva, não vi os sinais. Mas não é muito, só a porta, e o chefe* da garagem foi muito amável!

*o chefe: *the boss*

▶ Let's speak Portuguese

Here's your ten-point warm up: respond to the answers with a question, referring to the words in CAPITAL LETTERS.

Example: *Answer*: O PAULO está aqui. *Question*: Quem está aqui?

1 O telemóvel não está **NA MINHA BOLSA**.
2 **A AUTOESTRADA** é ao fim da estrada.
3 Há um autocarro **DENTRO DE VINTE MINUTOS**.
4 **O MEU MARIDO** queria falar com o senhor Pereira.
5 A ida a Lisboa custa **QUINZE EUROS**.
6 Não gosto da casa **PORQUE É VELHA**.
7 Vão à Inglaterra **DE CARRO**.
8 Fala inglês **MUITO DEVAGAR**.
9 **NÃO**, não gosto do preço.
10 **SIM**, estava contente com a escola.

While out shopping you are offered various items to buy. You'll take them all saying: 'Yes, I buy it' or 'Yes, I buy them'.

11	… a cerveja?	14	… as garrafas?
12	… o jornal?	15	… o Mercedes?
13	… os postais?	16	… a minha casa?

Here are four things you want to refer to, but you don't know how to say them in Portuguese. Explain them using the words you do know.

17	an au pair	19	a teacher
18	kennels	20	to be broke

Don't forget to mark your score! How's the star rating?

Answers

1 Onde está o telemóvel?
2 O que há ao fim da estrada?
3 Quando há um autocarro?
4 Quem queria falar com o senhor Pereira?
5 Quanto custa a ida a Lisboa?
6 Porque não gosta da casa?
7 Como vão à Inglaterra?
8 Como fala inglês?
9 Gosta do preço?
10 Estava contente com a escola?
11 Sim, compro-a.
12 Sim, compro-o.
13 Sim, compro-os.
14 Sim, compro-as.
15 Sim, compro-o.
16 Sim, compro-a.
17 Uma senhora que ajuda com o trabalho na casa.
18 Uma casa para os cães quando estamos de férias.
19 Uma senhora ou um senhor que trabalha numa escola.
20 Não temos dinheiro. Não temos um euro!

▶ Let's speak more Portuguese

In your own words

This exercise will teach you to express yourself freely. Use only the words you have learned so far.

Tell me in your own words that...

1 you bought a return ticket to Évora
2 you believe there is a train at 10.15
3 you have a seat in the non-smoking carriage
4 on (the) Monday you wouldn't mind going by bus to Mafra
5 you must take some photos for your company
6 this bus is 'chock-a-block'; you are going to take the other one
7 your car is coming on (the) Thursday; it is new but very cheap
8 your wife says: 'It's terrible, I don't like it (dele)'
9 she says the engine always overheats
10 hopefully you won't have problems

Answers
1 Comprei um bilhete de ida e volta para Évora.
2 Creio que há um comboio às dez e um quarto.
3 Tenho um lugar na carruagem de não fumadores.
4 Na segunda(-feira) queria ir a Mafra de autocarro.
5 Tenho de tirar umas fotos para a minha companhia.
6 Este autocarro está cheio. Vou apanhar o outro.
7 O meu carro vem na quinta(-feira). É novo mas muito barato.
8 A minha esposa diz: 'É terrível, não gosto dele'.
9 Diz que o motor está sempre muito quente.
10 Espero não ter problemas.

▶ Let's speak Portuguese – fast and fluently

Translate each section and check if it is correct, then cover up the answers and say the three or four sentences fast!

25 seconds per section for a silver star, 20 seconds for a gold star.

Some of the English is in 'Portuguese-speak' to help you.

A ticket to Lisbon, please, only one way.
How much? I am sorry, please speak more slowly.
Yes, I would like a seat in smoking.

Um bilhete para Lisboa se faz favor, só ida.
Quanto? Desculpe, fale mais devagar, se faz favor.
Sim, queria um lugar na carruagem de fumadores.

My wife is going to take a photo of the post box.
Here the post boxes are red like in (the) England.
Unfortunately, it is full.
What are we going to do with the letters?

A minha esposa vai tirar uma foto do marco.
Aqui os marcos são vermelhos como em Inglaterra.
Infelizmente, está cheio.
O que fazemos com as cartas?

We don't have (a) map of the Algarve.
My husband has (a) headache.
We have a problem. Our car is broken.

Não temos mapa do Algarve.
O meu marido tem dor de cabeça.
Temos um problema. O nosso carro está avariado.

Now say **all** the sentences in Portuguese without stopping and starting.

If you can do it in under one minute you are a fast and fluent winner!

But if you are not happy with your result – just try once more.

❯ Spot the keys

This time you plan a trip in the country and wonder about the weather. This is what you would ask:

You   **Desculpe, sabe que tempo temos hoje?**

Answer   *Não tenho a certeza, mas de acordo com a última previsão* **na televisão** *há uma frente lenta de baixas pressões que está a afastar-se até ao norte e espera-se que* **hoje o tempo** *esteja bastante* **quente***, isto é* **uns trinta graus, mas à noite** *esperamos umas tormentas* **e chuva**.

He isn't sure, but according to the TV, something slow is happening and it will be warm – 30°C – but with some (?) and rain in the night.

Test your progress

Translate into Portuguese – no looking at the previous pages!

1 I don't like this car, the other car was better.
2 How much does the ticket cost – one way only?
3 What did you say? Speak more slowly, please.
4 We hope to buy cheaper (more cheap) petrol in Portugal.
5 It is forbidden to smoke on the bus.
6 A yellow post box? I did not see (it).
7 Can I speak with the garage? We are (at) 30 km from Lisbon.
8 The train or the car on the (*na*) motorway goes more slowly?
9 He did not see the traffic lights, and now they are in (the) hospital.
10 There is a chemist's on the street, by the bus stop.
11 I would like two return tickets, non-smoking.
12 The problem with her (*dela*) is that she smokes too much.
13 He came here – to the end of the platform.
14 There is a lot of rain in England. I was happy to be in Portugal in March.
15 They say that the river is five minutes from the station.
16 If he does not give me the money, I go to the police.
17 This is the last petrol station. Do we have enough oil and water?
18 They come in July. I do not understand why (the) Pedro comes later.
19 I speak with him now. I have a mobile.
20 He didn't eat anything because he has a headache.

If you know all your words, you should score over 90%!

06

week six

This is your last week! Need I say more?

Day one

- Read **In the airport**.
- Listen to/Read **No aeroporto**.
- Read the **New words**. There are only 27!

Day two

- Read **No aeroporto**. Learn all the **New words**.
- Work with the **Flash words** and **Flash sentences**.

Day three

- Test yourself on the **Flash sentences**.
- Listen to/Read **Learn by heart**.

Day four

- No more **Good news grammar**! Have a look at the summary.
- Listen to/Read **Let's speak Portuguese**.

Day five

- Read **Say it simply**.
- Listen to/Read **Spot the keys**.

Day six

- Listen to/Read **Let's speak more Portuguese** (optional).
- Listen to/Read **Let's speak Portuguese – fast and fluently** (optional).
- Your last **Test your progress**! Go for it!

Day seven

Congratulations!

You have successfully completed the course and can now speak

Instant Portuguese!

In the airport

Tom and Kate are on their way home to Birmingham. They are in the departure lounge of Faro airport and meet an old friend.

Tom We have to work on Monday. What a bore! I would like to go to Italy or better to Hawaii. My company can wait and nobody is going to know where I am.

Kate And what are the people of my company going to say? They are going to wait for two days and then they are going to phone my mother. She certainly knows the number of my mobile. And then?

Tom Yes, yes, I know. Well, perhaps at Christmas a week's holiday in the snow or on a boat to Madeira. I am going to buy a newspaper. Kate! Here is Paulo Boa-morte!

Paulo Well, hello! What are you doing here? This is my wife, Nancy. How were your holidays – are they finished?

Kate The holidays? Great! We know the Algarve well now.

Paulo Next year you must go to Braga or to Viana do Castelo. My wife would like to buy a book about computers. Would you mind going with her and helping her, please? Mr Walker, you have a newspaper. What is happening with the football? And, would you like to have a drink?

(In a shop at the airport)

Kate I don't see anything. I don't like anything. Are you also going to England?

Nancy No, we are going to Lisbon to the house of Paulo's mother. Our children are always there during the holidays. We have a boy and three girls. Tomorrow we are going to take the train. It is cheaper.

Kate Your husband works in the Bank of Portugal, doesn't he?

Nancy Yes, his work is interesting but the pay is bad. We have a small apartment and an old car. We have to repair lots of things. My parents are in Los Angeles and I have a girlfriend in Florida and we write a lot of e-mails. I would like to go to America but it costs too much money.

┅➡ Page 78

▶ No aeroporto

Tom and Kate are on their way home to Birmingham. They are
in the departure lounge of Faro airport and meet an old friend.

Tom   Na segunda-feira temos de trabalhar. Que chatice! Queria
ir a Itália ou melhor, ao Havai. A minha companhia pode
esperar, e ninguém vai saber onde estou.

Kate   E o que vai dizer o pessoal da minha companhia? Vão
esperar dois dias e depois vão telefonar à minha mãe. É
certo que ela sabe o número do meu telemóvel. E depois?

Tom   Sim, sim, eu sei. Pois, talvez no Natal uma semana de
férias na neve, ou num barco para a Madeira. Vou comprar
um jornal. Kate! Aqui está o Paulo Boa-morte!

Paulo   Então, olá! O que fazem aqui? Esta é a minha esposa,
Nancy. Que tal as férias – já terminaram?

Kate   As férias? Magníficas! Agora conhecemos bem o Algarve.

Paulo   No ano que vem têm de ir para Braga ou para Viana do
Castelo. A minha esposa gostaria de comprar um livro
sobre informática. Importa-se de ir com ela e ajudar-la,
por favor? Sr Walker, tem um jornal. O que se passa com
o futebol? E, quer tomar uma bebida?

(Numa loja do aeroporto)

Kate   Não vejo nada. Não gosto de nada. A senhora também vai
para a Inglaterra?

Nancy   Não, vamos para Lisboa, à casa da mãe do Paulo. Os
nossos filhos estão sempre lá durante as férias. Temos um
filho e três filhas. Amanhã vamos apanhar o comboio. É
mais barato.

Kate   O seu marido trabalha no Banco de Portugal, não é?

Nancy   Sim, o trabalho dele é interessante, mas o salário é mau.
Temos um apartamento pequeno, e um carro velho.
Temos de consertar muitas coisas. Os meus pais estão
em Los Ângeles, e tenho uma amiga na Florida, e
escrevemos correios electrónicos. Queria ir aos Estados
Unidos mas custa muito dinheiro.

·····➡ Page 79

Kate	But you have a lovely house in Madeira.
Nancy	A house in Madeira? I have never been to Madeira. When we have holidays we go to the house of a friend in Nazaré.
Tom	Kate, come on, we have to go to the plane. Goodbye. What is the matter, Kate? What did Nancy say?
Kate	Wait, Tom, wait!

▶ New words

o aeroporto *the airport*
que chatice! *what a bore!*
esperar *(to) wait*
saber *(to) know*
dizer *(to) say*
o pessoal *the people, staff*
a mãe *the mother*
eu sei *I know*
ao Natal *at Christmas*
a neve *the snow*
o barco *the boat*
fazem *you/they do*
conhecemos *we know*
o livro *the book*
sobre *on, about*

importa-se? *would you mind?*
o que se passa? *what's happening?*
uma bebida *a drink*
vejo *I see*
o filho *the son*
a filha *the daughter*
o salário *the salary*
o apartamento *the apartment, flat*
escrevemos *we write*
o correio electrónico *the e-mail*
nunca *never*
espera! *wait!*

TOTAL NEW WORDS: 27
TOTAL PORTUGUESE WORDS LEARNED: 396
EXTRA WORDS: 79

GRAND TOTAL: 475

Kate	Mas a senhora tem uma casa bonita na Madeira.			
Nancy	Uma casa na Madeira? Nunca estive na Madeira. Quando temos férias vamos à casa dum amigo na Nazaré.			
Tom	Kate, vem, temos de ir para o avião. Adeus! O que disse a Nancy?			
Kate	Espera, Tom, espera!			

Good news grammar

As promised, there is no new grammar this week, just a summary of all the 30 **Instant** verbs which appear in the six weeks. Each one shows you the present tense with the most useful past tense forms in italics underneath. This is not for learning – you have done most of that – just for a quick check.

Basic form	I	You, he, she, it	We	You, they
ajudar*	ajudo	ajuda	ajudamos	ajudam
	ajudei	*ajudou*	*ajudámos*	*ajudaram*
beber*	bebo	bebe	bebemos	bebem
	bebi	*bebeu*	*bebemos*	*beberam*
chegar	chego	chega	chegamos	chegam
	cheguei	*chegou*	*chegámos*	*chegaram*
comer*	como	come	comemos	comem
	comi	*comeu*	*comemos*	*comeram*
comprar*	compro	compra	compramos	compram
	comprei	*comprou*	*comprámos*	*compraram*
compreender*	compreendo	compreende	compreendemos	compreendem
	compreendi	*compreendeu*	*compreendemos*	*compreenderam*
conhecer*	conheço	conhece	conhecemos	conhecem
	conheci	*conheceu*	*conhecemos*	*conheceram*
consertar*	conserto	conserta	consertamos	consertam
	consertei	*consertou*	*consertámos*	*consertaram*
crer	creio	crê	cremos	crêem
	cri	*creu*	*cremos*	*creram*
custar*		custa		custam
		custou		*custaram*
dar	dou	dá	damos	dão
	dei	*deu*	*demos*	*deram*
dizer	digo	diz	dizemos	dizem
	disse	*disse*	*dizemos*	*disseram*
escrever*	escrevo	escreve	escrevemos	escrevem
	escrevi	*escreveu*	*escrevemos*	*escreveram*
esperar*	espero	espera	esperamos	esperam
	esperei	*esperou*	*esperámos*	*esperaram*
estar	estou	está	estamos	estão
	estive	*esteve*	*estivemos*	*estiveram*
falar*	falo	fala	falamos	falam
	falei	*falou*	*falámos*	*falaram*
fazer	faço	faz	fazemos	fazem
	fiz	*fez*	*fizemos*	*fizeram*

fumar*	fumo	fuma	fumamos	fumam
	fumei	*fumou*	*fumámos*	*fumaram*
ir	vou	vai	vamos	vão
	fui†	*foi*	*fomos*	*foram*
poder	posso	pode	podemos	podem
	pude	*pôde*	*podemos*	*puderam*
querer	quero	quer	queremos	querem
	quis	*quis*	*quisemos*	*quiseram*
saber	sei	sabe	sabemos	sabem
	sabia	*sabia*	*sabíamos*	*sabiam*
ser	sou	é	somos	são
	fui†	*foi*	*fomos*	*foram*
	era	*era*	*éramos*	*eram*
telefonar*	telefono	telefona	telefonamos	telefonam
	telefonei	*telefonou*	*telefonámos*	*telefonaram*
ter	tenho	tem	temos	têm
	tive	*teve*	*tivemos*	*tiveram*
tomar*	tomo	toma	tomamos	tomam
	tomei	*tomou*	*tomámos*	*tomaram*
trabalhar*	trabalho	trabalha	trabalhamos	trabalham
	trabalhei	*trabalhou*	*trabalhámos*	*trabalharam*
ver	vejo	vê	vemos	vêem
	vi	*viu*	*vimos*	*viram*
vir	venho	vem	vimos	vêm
	vim	*veio*	*viemos*	*vieram*
viver*	vivo	vive	vivemos	vivem
	vivi	*viveu*	*vivemos*	*viveram*

* member of the Good Verbs Team

† Yes, *ir* and *ser* both have the *fui* pattern in the past – two for the price of one!

▶ Learn by heart

This is your last dialogue to **Learn by heart**. You now have six prize-winning party pieces, and a large store of everyday sayings which will be very useful.

Adeus!

Kate   Senhor Gomes, bom dia, sou a Kate Walker.
Estou no aeroporto.
Sim, as férias terminaram e o dinheiro também, infelizmente.
Tom queria falar com o senhor... e... adeus!

Tom   Olá, João! O quê? Como? Compra os dois?
A minha companhia tem o seu correio electrónico?
Excelente. Muito obrigado. No ano que vem?
A Kate queria ir à Itália, mas eu gosto de Portugal. Com a Edith Palmer?
Faz favor! Temos de ir para o avião. Adeus!

Say it simply

Here are two more exercises to practise using plain language:

1 You have just hired a car and notice a big scratch on the left, behind the door. You report it so as not to get the bill for it later.

2 You are Kate Walker at the airport, about to catch your flight home, when you realize that you have left some clothes behind in Room 32 of your hotel. You phone the hotel to ask the housekeeper to send the things on to you.

What would you say? Say it then write it down. Then see page 90.

▶ Spot the keys

Here's a final practice round. If you have the recording, close the book now. Find the keywords and try to get the gist of it. Then check on page 90.

This is what you might ask of a taxi driver:

You	Quanto tempo leva* para o aeroporto e quanto custa?
Answer	*Depende da hora em que vai sair. Normalmente chega nuns vinte minutos, mas se for na hora de ponta e houver muito trânsito e se houver um engarrafamento na ponte, deve calcular uns quarenta e cinco minutos. O preço está indicado no taxímetro. Normalmente custa entre vinte e vinte e cinco euros.*

(*how much time does it take?)

▶ Let's speak Portuguese

Here's a five-point warm up: answer these questions using the words in brackets:

1 Comprou o apartamento no Carvoeiro? (Sim, na segunda-feira)
2 Quantos anos trabalhou là? (durante três)
3 Quando falou com a companhia? (com ela, esta semana)
4 Por que tem de consertar o seu carro? (o meu carro, porque é velho)
5 Foi primeiro com a sua mãe? (não, com o cliente)

In your last exercise you are going to interpret again, this time telling your Portuguese friends what others have said in English. Each time say the whole sentence OUT LOUD, translating the English words.

6 A minha amiga disse (*that our holiday is over*).
7 Disse também (*that next year we go to America*).
8 A minha esposa queria dizer (*that she has a cold*).
9 O meu marido diz que não pode vir (*because he works on a ship*).
10 Não pode vir no Natal (*because his friend is coming*).
11 O meu amigo diz (*that you – feminine – are very good-looking*).
12 Também diz (*that he would like your* (o seu) *mobile number*).

Now do it once more – fast.

Answers

1 Sim, comprei-o na segunda-feira.
2 Trabalhei là durante três anos.
3 Falei com ela esta semana.
4 Tenho de consertar o meu carro porque é velho.
5 Não, primeiro foi com o cliente.
6 ...que as nossas férias terminaram.
7 ... que no ano que vem vamos aos Estados Unidos.
8 ... que tem uma constipação.
9 ... porque trabalha num barco.
10 ... porque vem o seu amigo.
11 ... que você/a sra é muito bonita.
12 ... que queria o número do seu telemóvel.

▶ Let's speak more Portuguese

In your own words

This exercise will teach you to express yourself freely. Use only the words you have learned so far.

Tell me in your own words that...

1 next week you have to work
2 you don't like to work; you'd rather have more leave
3 nobody knows that you are in (the) Madeira
4 your mother has the number of your mobile phone
5 your vacation in Portugal was wonderful
6 you did a lot of sightseeing and overeating
7 your friend Mr Lopes is on his way to Albufeira today
8 he is catching a train to Coimbra tomorrow
9 you and your wife must go to (the) America, because your father is ill
10 you would like to go to (the) Africa for Christmas, but by boat

Answers
1 Na semana que vem tenho de trabalhar.
2 Não gosto de trabalhar. Queria ter mais férias.
3 Ninguém sabe que estou na Madeira.
4 A minha mãe tem o número do meu telemóvel.
5 As férias em Portugal foram magníficas.
6 Vi muito e comi mais.
7 O meu amigo, o senhor Lopes, vai hoje para Albufeira.
8 Vai apanhar o comboio para Coimbra amanhã.
9 A minha esposa e eu temos de ir à América porque o meu pai está doente.
10 Queria ir à África no Natal, mas de barco.

▶ Let's speak Portuguese – fast and fluently

Translate each section and check if it is correct, then cover up the answers and say the three or four sentences fast!

30 seconds for a silver star, 20 seconds for a gold star.

The people in my company do not work a lot.
They write many e-mails on the computer.
And they always talk on the mobile phone.

O pessoal da minha companhia não trabalha muito.
Escrevem muitos correios electrónicos no computador.
E falam sempre ao telemóvel.

I know the Algarve and the Serra da Estrela very well.
Next year I would like to see Évora.
I must buy a book of the Pousadas of Portugal.

Conheço muito bem o Algarve e a Serra da Estrela.
Queria ver Évora no ano que vem.
Tenho de comprar um livro das pousadas de Portugal.

Well, hello, what are you doing here?
I need to repair my car and my flat. Both (the two) are very old.
The bill is terrible. Can you help me please – with 200 euros?

Então, olá! O que faz aqui?
Tenho de consertar o meu carro e o meu apartamento. Os dois são muito velhos.
A conta é terrível. Pode ajudar-me, se faz favor – com duzentos euros?

Now say **all** the sentences in Portuguese without stopping and starting.

If you can do it in under one minute you are a fast and fluent winner!

But if you are not happy with your result – just try once more.

Test your progress

I have crammed a lot into this last test – all 30 **Instant** verbs!
But don't panic – it looks worse than it is. Go for it – you'll do
brilliantly!

Translate into Portuguese:

1 I like writing letters because I have a new computer.
2 How are you? What is the matter? Can I help you?
3 The people in the company are rather boring.
4 I do not have the number of her mobile, I am sorry.
5 Do you like the Serra da Estrela? We had a lot of snow there this year.
6 The second case is in the bus. Did you see the black bag?
7 How many postcards did you write at Christmas? 88?
8 That's terrible. They did not eat for five days.
9 Why did you not telephone? We waited since yesterday.
10 When we arrive we have (take) a drink – or two.
11 Don't you know? The airport is always open – day and night.
12 I know that he did it.
13 I have worked (for) many years but never on a boat.
14 I have given my car to my son. He is very pleased.
15 Your mother is very nice and makes (a) great cod (dish).
16 Do you live in a house or a flat in Vilamoura?
17 We must work many hours. Four daughters cost a lot of money.
18 Can the garage repair this? I think so (that yes).
19 I know him. He always goes shopping with the dog.
20 Who said one cannot smoke here?
21 We go by (de) plane to Dallas. Then we go by (de) car to Las Vegas.
22 I would like to speak with the sales assistant. He did not give me the bill.
23 We drank your wine but we have come today with two more bottles.
24 I am sorry, but **Instant Portuguese** has now finished.

Check your answers on page 89. Then enter your final score on
the **Progress chart** and – write out your certificate!

answers

How to score

From a total of 100%
- Subtract 1% for each wrong or missing word.
- Subtract 1% for the wrong form of the verb. Example *we are* estou (estamos).
- Subtract 1% every time you mix up the present and the past tenses.

There are no penalties for:
- wrong use of all those little words like: **a, o, os, as, da, do, na, no, em, este, neste, me, mim, ele, ela, nos, eles,** etc.
- wrong endings of adjectives like: **um trabalho boa (bom)**
- wrong use of **ser** and **estar**
- omission of **o** and **a** which appear here and there and don't really translate
- wrong or different word order
- wrong spelling or missing accents – as long as you can *say* the word:
  Examples: **dinhero (dinheiro), e (é), sao (são)**

100% LESS YOUR PENALTIES WILL GIVE YOU YOUR WEEKLY SCORE

For each test, correct your mistakes. Then read the corrected answers out loud twice.

Week 1: Test your progress

1 O meu nome é Peter Smith.
2 Olá, sou Paulo e esta é Helen.
3 Sou de Lisboa. E o senhor?
4 A Maria é uma boa amiga.
5 Vou sempre para casa em Junho.

6 Trabalhamos no Estoril em Agosto.

7 Trabalhei em Nova Iorque em Março.

8 O que é que faz? Trabalha em informática?

9 Estive em Londres com os filhos.

10 Um momento, se faz favor. O que é? Custa muito dinheiro?

11 A casa tem telefone? Não, infelizmente não.

12 Bom dia, é o senhor Soares do Porto?

13 Trabalhei para uma companhia americana.

14 Agora tenho um trabalho melhor. Trabalho para três bancos grandes.

15 Luís! Vamos para Faro?

16 A minha esposa é americana também. Ela é de Boston.

17 Temos lugares bons no avião.

18 Tenho um Mercedes? Não, infelizmente não!

19 A minha amiga trabalha, mas não muito.

20 Vou de férias com a Teresa. Infelizmente, é chata.

YOUR SCORE: _____ %

Week 2: Test your progress

1 Onde há um telefone? À direita?

2 Podemos comer rissóis aqui? Há lugares para quatro?

3 Tem uma mesa? Às oito e meia? Somos seis.

4 Vamos para Lagos, está bem?

5 Pode consertar o Ford? Está avariado.

6 Estamos no quarto. Onde está (o senhor/a senhora)?

7 Os pastéis de bacalhau estão excelentes. Posso comer muitos.

8 Posso lhe perguntar? Tem uma companhia pequena. É em Texas?

9 Não podemos ir de férias em Julho. Não temos dinheiro.

10 Onde está o empregado? Tem a minha conta?

11 Onde são os lavabos? À esquerda?

12 A Maria e eu queríamos ir a Évora – sem maridos.

13 Desculpe, só tenho trinta e cinco euros e um cartão de crédito.

14 Três euros e dez cêntimos para uma sandes? É muito cara.

15 Estive em Loulé por uma noite. Custa menos em Novembro.

16 A Manuela é muito bonita. Onde trabalha? Muito perto?

17 Está bem! Tomamos quatro chás com leite, se faz favor.

18 Londres não é bonito em Novembro.

19 Trabalhei um pouco com computadores (em informática). Não é fácil.

20 Quantos meses estivemos aqui? Dez?

YOUR SCORE: _____ %

Week 3: Test your progress

1 Podemos comprar selos na tabacaria?
2 Trabalhou no cabeleireiro? Não, na farmácia.
3 A Maria era muito amável, como sempre.
4 Meu Deus! Todas os multibancos estão avariados!
5 Hoje é um dia bastante bom.
6 O jornal inglês não é barato.
7 Creio que vi uma tinturaria no centro comercial.
8 Até que horas tem de trabalhar? Até às oito?
9 Quando temos de ir? Não posso ir até mais tarde.
10 Em Novembro sempre faz mau tempo em Manchester.
11 O que comprou? Seis garrafas de vinho tinto? Excelente!
12 O tamanho quatro: o que é isso em inglês?
13 Está muito frio nesta casa. Tenho de comprar alguma coisa.
14 Primeiro fui fazer compras e depois comemos com amigos.
15 Ontem comprámos uma televisão nova. E hoje está avariada.
16 Comprou uma mala preta, não vermelha.
17 Tudo era muito caro, então não comprámos nada.
18 Quem é o vendedor? Onde há leite?
19 Não temos a T-shirt em verde e ao mesmo preço. Desculpe.
20 Queria comprar alguma coisa. Alguma coisa para mim, mas não muito cara.

YOUR SCORE: _____ %

Week 4: Test your progress

1 O que disse? Disse: para quem são as batatas fritas?
2 Pode vir à nossa casa? Na semana que vem?
3 Ela diz que a saída da loja é em cima detrás do bar.
4 Disse que ele foi para a Inglaterra?
5 O que quer? É que estou doente e não posso trabalhar.
6 Podia ajudar-me por favor? Há um médico aqui?
7 Ele vai ao encontro marcado sem sapatos? Não se pode fazer isso.
8 Conheço Lúcia Pereira. É uma senhora muito interessante.
9 Ninguém pode beber quinze cervejas numa noite. Não é possível.
10 Gosto muito da sobremesa. Queria o gelado.
11 Creio que é uma coisa importante, mas não temos tempo.
12 Terminámos e agora temos de ir para Braga.
13 Como muitas saladas. O que come (o senhor/a senhora)?
14 Como gosta do peixe? Sem alho?
15 O nome deste legume: como se diz em português?

16 Não há lojas em frente da igreja, ou atrás. O que vamos fazer?
17 A companhia telefonou. Um sr Lopes disse que não era importante.
18 Certamente têm água com gás. Sempre têm.
19 Diz que tem dores desde ontem.
20 Tenho uma constipação. Não posso ir para a Inglaterra hoje.

> **YOUR SCORE: _____ %**

Week 5: Test your progress

1 Não gosto deste carro, o outro carro era melhor.
2 Quanto custa o bilhete – só ida?
3 O que disse? Fale mais devagar, se faz favor.
4 Esperamos comprar gasolina mais barata em Portugal.
5 É proibido fumar no autocarro.
6 Uma caixa de correio amarela? Não (o) sabia.
7 Posso falar com a garagem? Estamos a trinta quilómetros de Lisboa.
8 O comboio ou o carro na autoestrada vai mais devagar?
9 Não viu os sinais, e agora estão no hospital.
10 Há uma farmácia na rua, à paragem de autocarros.
11 Queria dois bilhetes de ida e volta, não fumadores.
12 O problema dela é que fuma demasiado.
13 Veio aqui, ao fim da linha.
14 Há muita chuva na Inglaterra. Estive contente de estar em Portugal em Março.
15 Dizem que o rio está a cinco minutos da estação.
16 Se não me dá o dinheiro, vou à polícia.
17 Esta é a última bomba de gasolina. Temos óleo e água suficientes?
18 Vêm em Julho. Não compreendo por que o Pedro vem mais tarde.
19 Falo com ele agora. Tenho um telemóvel.
20 Não comeu nada porque tem uma dor de cabeça.

> **YOUR SCORE: _____ %**

Week 6: Test your progress

1 Gosto de escrever cartas porque tenho um computador novo.
2 Como está? O que tem? Posso ajudá-lo/la?
3 O pessoal na companhia é bastante chato.
4 Não tenho o número do seu telemóvel, desculpe.

5 Gosta da Serra da Estrela? Tivemos muita neve ali este ano.
6 A segunda mala está no autocarro. Viu o saco preto?
7 Quantos postais escreveu no Natal? Oitenta e oito?
8 Isso é terrível. Não comeram durante cinco dias.
9 Por que não telefonou? Esperámos desde ontem.
10 Quando chegamos tomamos uma bebida – ou duas.
11 Não sabe? O aeroporto está sempre aberto – dia e noite.
12 Sei que ele o fez.
13 Trabalhei durante muitos anos mas nunca num barco.
14 Dei o meu carro ao meu filho. Está muito contente.
15 A sua mãe é muito amável e faz um bacalhau excelente.
16 Vive numa casa ou num apartamento em Vilamoura?
17 Temos de trabalhar muitas horas. Quatro filhas custam muito dinheiro.
18 A garagem pode consertar isso? Creio que sim.
19 Conheço-o. Vai fazer compras sempre com o cão.
20 Quem disse que não se pode fumar aqui?
21 Vamos a Dallas de avião. Depois vamos de carro a Las Vegas.
22 Queria falar com o vendedor. Não me deu a conta.
23 Bebemos o seu vinho mas viemos hoje com mais duas garrafas.
24 Sinto muito, mas **Instant Portuguese** agora terminou.

YOUR SCORE: _____ %

Week 6: Say it simply

1 Desculpe, há um problema com o carro. Pode vir, se faz favor? Isto, detrás da porta, aqui à esquerda. Eu não o fiz. Não queria ter um problema mais tarde.

2 Olá, bom dia, sou Kate Walker. O número do meu quarto é o trinta e dois. Telefono do aeroporto. Tenho umas coisas no meu quarto e agora vamos a Birmingham. Sinto muito, mas pode ajudar-me, se faz favor? Tenho de ter as coisas. O hotel sabe onde vivo em Birmingham. Muito obrigada.

Week 6: Spot the keys

It depends on the time you are going to leave. Normally it takes about 20 minutes but if you leave in the rush hour and if there is a lot of traffic and a traffic jam on the bridge, you have to calculate some 45 minutes. The price is shown on the meter. Normally it costs between €20 and €25.

how to use the flash cards

The **Flash cards** have been voted the best part of this course! Learning words and sentences can be tedious, but with flash cards it's quick and good fun.

This is what you do:

When the **Day-by-day guide** tells you to use the cards, cut them out. There are 22 **Flash words** and 10 **Flash sentences** for each week. Each card has the week number on it, so you won't cut out too many cards at a time or muddle them up later on.

First, try to learn the words and sentences by looking at both sides of the cards. Then, when you have a rough idea, start testing yourself. That's the fun bit. Look at the English, say the Portuguese, and then check. Make two piles: 'correct' and 'wrong' or 'don't know'. When all the cards are used up, start again with the 'wrong' pile and try to whittle it down until you get all of them right. You can also play it 'backwards' by starting with the Portuguese face up.

Keep the cards in a little box or put an elastic band around them. Take them with you on the bus, the train, to the hairdresser's or the dentist's. If you find the paper too flimsy, photocopy the words and sentences onto card before cutting them up. You could also buy some plain card and stick them on or simply copy them out.

The 22 **Flash words** for each week are there to start you off. Convert the rest of the **New words** to **Flash words**, too. It's well worth it!

FLASH CARDS for Instant LEARNING:
DON'T LOSE THEM – USE THEM!

temos [1]	vamos [1]
vou [1]	estive [1]
para [1]	trabalho [1]
trabalhei [1]	agora [1]
o dinheiro [1]	tenho [1]
tem [1]	sempre [1]

we go, we [1] are going, let's go	we have [1]
I was, have been [1]	I go [1]
I work [1]	to, for [1]
now [1]	I (have) worked [1]
I have [1]	the money [1]
always [1]	he/she/it has, you (s.) have [1]

é [1]	também [1]
de férias [1]	infelizmente [1]
o meu nome é [1]	desculpe [1]
com [1]	custa [1]
o telemóvel [1]	melhor [1]
à direita [2]	à esquerda [2]

also, too [1]	he/she/it is, you are [1]
unfortunately [1]	on holiday [1]
excuse me, sorry [1]	my name is [1]
with [1]	it costs [1]
the mobile phone [1]	better [1]
on/to the left [2]	on/to the right [2]

alguma coisa **2**	caro/a **2**
perto **2**	comer **2**
quanto…? **2**	onde…? **2**
o pequeno almoço **2**	excelente **2**
há **2**	ir **2**
a conta **2**	logo **2**

expensive **2**	something **2**
(to) eat **2**	near **2**
where…? **2**	how much…? **2**
great, marvellous **2**	the breakfast **2**
(to) go **2**	there is, there are **2**
then, later **2**	the bill **2**

muito ²	posso ²
podemos ²	queríamos ²
menos ²	o marido ²
mau ²	os lavabos ²
primeiro ³	um multibanco ³
a tabacaria ³	o Correio ³

I can, may **2**	very **2**
we would like **2**	we can, may **2**
the husband **2**	less **2**
the toilets **2**	bad **2**
a cashpoint **3**	first **3**
the Post Office **3**	the tobacconist **3**

3	3
comprar	os selos
3 depois	**3** talvez
3 queria	**3** tenho de
3 até	**3** aberto/a
3 mais tarde	**3** os ovos
3 bastante	**3** ontem

the stamps **3**	(to) buy **3**
perhaps **3**	afterwards, then **3**
I have to, must **3**	I would like (to) **3**
open **3**	until **3**
the eggs **3**	later **3**
yesterday **3**	enough, rather **3**

3 quem	**3** um jornal
3 a farmácia	**3** a manteiga
3 creio	**3** novo
4 a água	**4** alguém
4 em cima	**4** em frente (de)
4 atrás (de)	**4** o peixe

3 a newspaper	**3** who
3 the butter	**3** the pharmacy
3 new	**3** I believe
4 someone	**4** the water
4 in front (of)	**4** above, upstairs
4 the fish	**4** behind

4 está bem	4 como…?
4 a saída	4 gosto (de)
4 ninguém	4 o nosso
4 certamente	4 terminar
4 uma constipação	4 um copo
4 uma coisa	4 vir

4	4
how…?	all right, OK
4	**4**
I like	the exit
4	**4**
our	nobody
4	**4**
(to) finish	sure, certainly
4	**4**
a glass	a cold
4	**4**
(to) come	a thing, matter

4 **conheço**	4 **beber**
4 **um cão**	4 **a dor**
5 **a estação**	5 **anda, vem!**
5 **a paragem**	5 **ali**
5 **em baixo**	5 **o marco**
5 **fazer**	5 **porque…?**

drink, to drink 4	**I know** 4
the pain 4	**a dog** 4
come, come on! 5	**the station** 5
there 5	**the stop** 5
the post box 5	**below, downstairs** 5
why…? 5	**to do, make** 5

5	5
cheio/a	a outro/a outra

5	5
o carro	a rua

5	5
se	a gasolina

5	5
a garagem	quente

5	5
a chuva	contente

5	5
o problema	compreendo

the other 5	full 5
the street 5	the car 5
the petrol 5	if 5
hot 5	the garage 5
happy, content 5	the rain 5
I understand 5	the problem 5

5	5
o bilhete	o/a último/a

6	6
o aeroporto	esperar

6	6
dizer	no Natal

6	6
a neve	que chatice!

6	6
o barco	importa-se?

6	6
vejo	nunca

5 the last	**5** the ticket
6 (to) wait	**6** the airport
6 at Christmas	**6** (to) say
6 what a bore!	**6** the snow
6 would you mind?	**6** the boat
6 never	**6** I see

6 escrevemos	6 espera!
6 o apartamento	6 eu sei
6 saber	6 o pessoal
6 sobre	6 conhecemos
6 o livro	6 o barco
6 fazem	6 o correio electrônico

wait! [6]	we write [6]
I know [6]	the flat, apartment [6]
the people, staff [6]	(to) know [6]
we know [6]	on, about [6]
the boat [6]	the book [6]
the e-mail [6]	they do, you do [6]

Vamos para Lisboa. 1

Estive no Porto. 1

em trabalho 1

Tenho uma casa. 1

Temos dois filhos. 1

A minha esposa tem um Mercedes. 1

Custa muito dinheiro. 1

Trabalho em Londres. 1

Trabalhei muitos anos. 1

O trabalho é bom. 1

We go/Let's go to Lisbon. 1

I was/have been in Oporto. 1

on business/
for my company 1

I have a house. 1

We have two children. 1

My wife has a Mercedes. 1

It costs a lot of money. 1

I work in London. 1

I (have) worked
many years. 1

The work is good. 1

Tem um quarto? 2

Onde é o café? 2

Quanto custa? 2

Há um banco aqui? 2

Queríamos ir para Lagos. 2

às dez e meia 2

A conta, se faz favor. 2

Tenho um cartão de crédito. 2

Não posso ir. 2

A que horas podemos comer? 2

Do you have a room? [2]

Where is the café? [2]

How much does it cost? [2]

Is there a bank here? [2]

We would like to go to Lagos. [2]

at half past ten [2]

The bill, please. [2]

I have a credit card. [2]

I cannot go. [2]

At what time can we eat? [2]

Vou fazer compras. **3**

Tenho de ir fazer compras. **3**

Faz mau tempo. **3**

Sinto muito. **3**

Comprei demasiado. **3**

Não importa. **3**

Queria comprar… **3**

Fui ao supermercado. **3**

Temos de comprar… **3**

Vi o futebol. **3**

I'm going shopping. **3**

I have to/must go shopping. **3**

It's bad weather. **3**

I'm very sorry. **3**

I (have) bought too much. **3**

No problem. **3**

I would like to buy… **3**

I went to the supermarket. **3**

We have to/must buy… **3**

I saw the football. **3**

Alguém telefonou. 4

Não disse para qué. 4

É uma coisa importante. 4

Na semana que vem 4
temos tempo.

Isso é possível. 4

Gosto muito. 4

Não gosto do alho. 4

Gosta do hotel? 4

Podia ajudar-me, 4
por favor?

Como se diz…em 4
português?

Someone phoned. 4

He/she didn't say 4
what for.

It's an important matter. 4

Next week we have time. 4

That's possible. 4

I like it a lot. 4

I don't like (the) garlic. 4

Do you (does he/she) 4
like the hotel?

Could you help me, 4
please?

How does one say ... 4
in Portuguese?

dois bilhetes de 5
ida e volta

Fale mais devagar, 5
se faz favor.

Quando há um comboio? 5

Vou fazer alguma coisa. 5

Estou muito contente. 5

Esperamos que sim. 5

Onde é a estrada? 5

Por que o compra? 5
Porque gosto.

Falo só um pouco 5
de português.

Se há um bilhete, tomo-o. 5

two return tickets 5

Speak more slowly, 5
please.

When is there a train? 5

I am going to do 5
something.

I am very happy. 5

We hope so. 5

Where is the main road? 5

Why are you buying it? 5
Because I like it!

I only speak a little 5
Portuguese.

If there is a ticket, 5
I'll take it.

Que tal as suas férias? [6]

Importa-se me ajudar? [6]

Importa-se me dar…? [6]

O que se passa com…? [6]

Vamos tomar uma bebida. [6]

Nunca fui para Lisboa. [6]

Temos de trabalhar.
Que chatice! [6]

Esperei durante uma
semana. [6]

O que fez? [6]

Têm um apartamento.
Eu sei. [6]

How are/were your holidays? 6

Would you mind helping me? 6

Would you mind giving me...? 6

What's the matter with...? 6

Let's go and have a drink. 6

I never went to Lisbon. 6

We must work. What a bore! 6

I waited for a week. 6

What did you do? 6

They have a flat. I know that. 6

This is to certify
that

....

has successfully completed
a six-week course of

Instant Portuguese

with .... results

Date　　　　　　　　　　　　*Instructor*